Travels with Surly: Pedalling The Mother Road

About the author

Mick Dolan retired from the Irish Defence Forces in 2014, after over thirty-five years service at home and abroad. A well-travelled soldier, he served on United Nations- mandated missions in the Middle East, Central America, and the Balkans and also with an Irish Aid Organisation in Africa in the 1990s. Retirement has afforded him the opportunity to undertake more protracted tours and this solo, self-supported touring has included a TransAmerica Tour in 2014, The Wild Atlantic Way in 2015 and the Camino de Santiago de Compostela in 2012. He has also competed in the TransAtlanticWay Race in Ireland in 2017. This is his second book.

Also

Travels with Surly: Cycling across the USA
Available from Amazon – or directly from Author
Contact the Author at **mickdolan6@gmail.com**

Travels with Surly: Pedalling The Mother Road

By

Mick Dolan

Ballyglass Books
Kiltimagh
Co. Mayo, Ireland

Copyright © Mick Dolan

Mickl Dolan has asserted his right under the Copyright, Designs and Patents Act 1988 to be identified as the author of this work

This book is sold subject to the condition that it shall not, by way of trade or otherwise, be lent, resold, hired out, or otherwise circulated without the publisher's prior consent in any form of binding or cover other than that in which it is published and without a similar condition being imposed on the subsequent purchaser

First published in Ireland in 2017 by Ballyglass Books

Cover design by
Createspace.com

Note: This work represents the personal observations of the author, supplemented, where applicable, by historical vignettes from diverse open sources. Special mention must be made of John Steinbeck's work, The Grapes of Wrath, a Penguin Classic

For all those in search of Adventure

The difference between an Adventure and a Road Trip is the degree to which the outcome is pre-determined. This was a Road Trip
— Author

Table of Contents

Chapter			Page
Chapter 1	...	Introduction	9
Chapter 2	...	Illinois – The Prairie State	23
Chapter 3	...	Missouri – "Show Me" State	41
Chapter 4	...	Oklahoma – The Sooner State	65
Chapter 5	...	Texas – The Lone Star State	113
Chapter 6	...	New Mexico – Land of Enchantment	143
Chapter 7	...	Arizona – Grand Canyon State	173
Chapter 8	...	California – The Golden State	217
Chapter 9	...	Epilogue – The Road to the Airport	247
Appendix	...	Packing List	251
		Accommodation	255

Chapter 1

Introduction

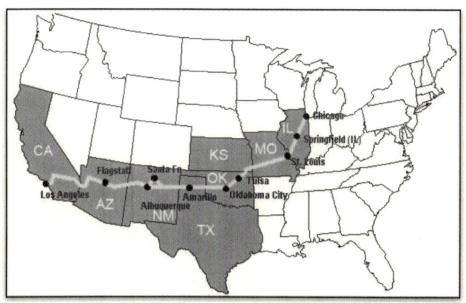

Route 66 (http://route66.backroadsplanet.com)

Route 66's rich history is much more than the story of the road itself. To the casual and accidental historian that I am, it was an artery of transportation, stretching two thousand four hundred miles, through eight states and three time-zones, across two-thirds of the continent. But I discovered that it was an agent of social transformation and a living – though endangered – remnant of America's past. It winds from the shores of Lake Michigan across the agricultural fields of Illinois, to the rolling hills of the Missouri Ozarks, through the mining towns of Kansas, across Oklahoma where the woodlands of the East meet the open plains of the West, to the open ranch lands of Texas, the mesa lands of New Mexico and Arizona, to the Mojave Desert, and finally to the "land of milk and honey" – the metropolis of Los Angeles and the shores of the Pacific Ocean, at Santa Monica Pier. Route 66 demonstrates the historical change that transformed the lives of people, their communities, and the nation. It connects the past and the present as well as the East and the West. It is a route familiar to anyone even vaguely interested in travel in the United States or population movement during the Great Depression or in the aftermath of the Second World War. My feeling, having cycled it over thirty-seven days from Chicago IL to Santa Monica CA, is that, while Route 66 is the living embodiment of motor transport in the USA, it would be a mistake to ignore the contribution of mining, agriculture, oil and war to the development of communities along its path.

From the distance of hindsight, I wonder what I missed – two thousand four hundred miles should have demonstrated ample differences in culture, but I could see little. The "settled" population I encountered along the way was predominantly white, god-fearing and, overwhelmingly, Republican. Undertaking a similar journey in Europe would entail travelling from Western France to Moscow, with all the cultural shifts that would be evident along the way. Perhaps the road itself was the culture, defining those who had taken up residence along its stretch or who had been fundamentally influenced by its passing through their lives. The often-romanticised Mother Road generates nostalgia, whether for the freedom it allowed or as a reminder of the misery experienced by those who fled the Dust Bowl poverty. Even that event, portrayed by John Steinbeck in his novel, The Grapes of Wrath, manages to convey the indomitable nature of the human spirit and the resilience of those who had no option but to take to the road.

From 1933 to 1938 thousands of unemployed male youths from virtually every state were put to work as labourers on road gangs to pave the final stretches of the road and the result of this monumental effort was the declaration, in 1938, that the Chicago-to-Los Angeles highway was "continuously paved". Completion of this all-weather capability on the eve of World War II was particularly significant to the nation's war effort. The West was singled out as ideal for military training bases in part because of its geographic isolation and especially because it offered consistently dry weather for air and field manoeuvres. The War Department needed improved highways for rapid mobilization and to promote national defence during peacetime. Route 66 allowed that access – the Frontier was finally gone.

Increased disposable income and access to motor transport following the Second World War – along with leisure time – allowed overland travel to be enjoyed by more and more Americans. Thousands of soldiers, sailors, and airmen who had received military training in California, Arizona, New Mexico, Oklahoma, and Texas realised that the harsh winters of Chicago, New York City, and Boston could be left behind for the "barbecue culture" of the Southwest and the West. Route 66 facilitated relocation for many. Familiar, from their wartime training, with the attractions "way out there", they could forge a life in a better climate. As I paralleled the Interstates, on the Historic Route 66, U-Haul vans and trailers moving the lives of Americans in both directions were ever-present. Ironically, that which made Route 66 popular – the desire for speed and ease of movement – was primarily responsible for its demise. Excessive truck use during World War II and the growth of the automobile industry immediately following the war brought great pressure to bear on America's highways. The national highway system had fallen into significant disrepair and virtually all roads were no longer functionally fit for purpose and dangerous because of narrow pavements and structural features, such as bridges, that reduced carrying capacity.

Dwight D. Eisenhower's second term in the White House in the mid-1950's, increased federal sponsorship for an interstate system of divided highways. He'd been very impressed with the strategic value of Hitler's autobahns in Germany. "During World War II," he recalled later, "I saw the superlative system of German national highways crossing that country and offering the possibility, often lacking in the United States, to drive with speed and safety at the same time." The Federal Aid Highway Act of 1956 was provided to underwrite the cost of the national interstate and defence highway system. By 1970, nearly all segments of original Route 66 were bypassed by a modern four-lane highway.

In many respects, the physical remains of Route 66 mirror the evolution of highway development in the United States from a basic mixture of state and country roads into a complex of uniform, well-designed interstate expressways. Various alignments of the legendary road, many still detectable, illustrate the evolution of road engineering from coexistence with the surrounding landscape to domination of it. Route 66 symbolized a renewed spirit of optimism after economic catastrophe and global war. Often called, "The Main Street of America", it linked a remote and under-populated region with two vital 20th century cities – Chicago and Los Angeles.

Now, Route 66 has developed into a leisure route for those, like me, who want to experience what early motor travellers experienced. Those seeking the more active, post-war speed and mobility, travel on their Harleys, or in their Corvettes, conjuring up images of Kerouac's On The Road or the sixties television serial Route 66. It's all about adventure.

In the US, Highways that run north-south have odd numbers while those running east-west have even numbers. Route 66 was considered the "super-highway," when conceived in 1926, and differed from other highway systems in that it didn't go north-south or east-west. Instead, it took a diagonal route, linking small towns across America and providing farmers with a route to market. It offered unprecedented freedom to travel across the American West in relative safety. A cowboy on horseback, as I discovered along the way, will cover thirty-five miles in a ten-hour working day. The internal combustion engine didn't tire so the badlands of New Mexico and Arizona were no longer significant barriers. They were now opened up as crossable.

John Ford directed the movie of Steinbeck's classic The Grapes of Wrath in 1939 and immortalized Route 66 in the American consciousness. The migration of two hundred thousand people – the largest ever movement of American people – to California to escape the Dust Bowl of the Midwest, created the idea that the highway was the "road to opportunity." Re-examining the Great Depression years, contemporary writers found that thousands of disillusioned immigrants returned home within months of reaching the Golden State. Of the dispossessed and hopeless who journeyed west to California beginning in the early 1930s, it seems that less than 16,000 people from the Dust Bowl proper actually ended up in California. The historical accuracy did nothing to dispel the accepted story of the route. While the importance of Route 66 to emigrating "Dust Bowlers" during the Depression years received wide publicity, less is known about the importance of the highway to those who opted to eke out a living in economically devastated Kansas, Oklahoma, West Texas, and New Mexico. During this time, U.S. Highway 66 and other major roads in America had major links to Roosevelt's revolutionary New Deal programs for work relief and economic recovery. Road improvements and maintenance work were central features of the New Deal's Civilian Conservation Corps (CCC) and Works Project Administration (WPA) programs. Route 66 seems to have impacted more Americans on Federal work relief than people who used it during the famous exodus to California.

In February 1942, It was announced that existing rail and bus transit facilities could accommodate only a small fraction of the ten million workers required to operate the defence plants. The rest would have to move in private automobiles. The net result of this mass migration in unprecedented numbers was the loss of more than one million people from the metropolitan northeast between 1940 and 1943. The population of Pacific Coast States – California, Oregon, and Washington – grew by almost forty percent and Route 66 played a critical role in this movement of Americans to meet the demands of war. It was invaluable in transporting troops, equipment and products across the vast West to California, where the government established multiple industries and armed force bases. When the war ended in 1945, the Mother Road served to transport thousands of troops home.

In the affluence of post-war America, the misery experienced by John Steinbeck's characters seemed to fade from memory and what remained was a map – a directory for the adventurous. Perhaps more than any other American highway, Route 66 symbolized a new positive outlook that spread through the nation's economic recovery. For thousands of returning servicemen and their families, Route 66 was more than just a highway. It became an emblem of free-spirited independence linking the United States across the Rocky Mountain divide to the Pacific Ocean. Their population's geographical horizons had been exploded through relocation during the war and long-distance travel was no longer confined to the adventurous few.

Almost immediately, the growth of the tourist industry gave rise to countless tourist courts, motels, service stations, garages and diners. But the excessive truck travel during World War II and the ever expanding automobile industry had left the Highway in appalling conditions, with narrow pavements and poor road conditions and, by the time Eisenhower's Federal Highway Act funded the final section of Route 66 in Williams, Arizona in 1984, Main Street, USA was a memory. Route 66 was decommissioned on June 27, 1985 and its signs were removed. The Mother Road was almost lost. Even to this day, it appears on very few current maps. Most states have installed Historic Route 66 signs along portions of the road, but they rarely give exit directions where the road so very often veers off from the interstate highways. This is a bonus for the traveller who gets on at the start. Traffic is light – mostly tourist in search of the iconic landmarks that once provided an escape from normal life for vacationers. Today, the route is a living thing with sights and sounds changing constantly with the emergence of new businesses and development along the old highway.

Route 66 Historical Associations and private groups have done a lot to preserve many of the vintage treasures and landmarks. Signs along the vintage road – billboards and motel banners – indicate icons of history that are preserved, though their buildings are long gone. The landscape quickly changes from the hustle and bustle of metropolitan area, to quiet meandering roads, to tall grass prairies, to deserts where you feel as if you might be the only person left on earth.

When the Adventure Cycling Association (ACA) had mapped the route, I felt it would be a once-in-a-lifetime opportunity to revisit the US with my trusty bicycle, Surly. I'd used their maps in 2014 to get from San Francisco to Boston – and hadn't gotten irretrievably lost – so I would follow them again, to visit new states.

The blurb was seductive. My previous trip had been extremely educational, both in terms of personal development and cycle-touring. It had been an adventure. The difference between a cycling adventure and a road trip lies, I believe, in the degree of certainty of the outcome. I'd survived the last one of over four thousand five hundred miles. This one – including the "optional extra" from Santa Monica to San Francisco to meet with Henry and Danielle, with whom I'd connected on my last trip – was just a shade over three thousand. I would make up for the unrealised dreams of the previous visit. Diners, motels and bars would welcome me. Fellow travellers would abound and, because I was now aware of my strengths and weaknesses, I would be better prepared.

The ACA promised a certain satisfaction as I would whiz past the many gas stations found in the towns and cities I would visit. Bicycle Route 66 travels west on bike paths, county roads and state, federal and interstate highways. It doesn't always follow Historic Route 66. Deviations from the route were made based on present-day conditions. Interstates 55, 44, 40 and 10 replaced the original route and killed many towns along the way. The official start location on Lake Michigan in Grant Park at Buckingham Fountain allows the use of multiple bike paths and trails along with city streets out of the congestion of Chicago to meet up with Historic Route 66 in Elwood. A short distance later, the route begins its parallel path with I-55 passing through the state capital city of Springfield as well as many smaller communities.

D-2 Getting to Chicago

The pre-departure period was much calmer than my last trans-Atlantic flight. From my flight to San Francisco and back from Boston in 2014, I knew that:

- Pre-clearance at Dublin works fine
- My ESTA document in my new passport was in order
- I was within weight limits
- Surly would survive the flight in the plastic bag from Wiggle.co.uk.

I'd lightened my load a little, from the packing list of 2014, through a few small changes. The new Ortlieb panniers were waterproof and had proved themselves on Ireland's Wild Atlantic Way in 2015. I didn't have to line them with plastic bags to keep my stuff dry. My foot had, over long distances, caused me some nervous pain on the last trip. In an effort to avoid this, I'd taken the radical step of dispensing with SPD clipless pedals in favour of MTB pedals, with their little studs to grip the sole of a shoe. Time would tell if this was a good idea or not, but it allowed me travel with just Columbia Goretex shoes and a pair of sandals. One change of on-bike clothing and a single set of off-bike clothing would do. There was little likelihood of being invited to a formal dinner! Availability of water would not be a significant issue until I got to Oklahoma, at the earliest, so I would save myself some weight there.

My panniers would be packed in the same way as before – front right carried my tool box, maps, rain jacket and first aid. Front left held my food and cooking equipment. The rear left pannier held my sleeping bag, off-bike clothes and warm jacket while the rear right housed my sleeping mat and on-bike stuff. All in all, I had enough storage space – and the extra bungies I carried would secure anything else I needed to strap on. The tent – a change from last time – occupied the rear rack. This time, I brought a free-standing two-man tent. This would remove the problem of not being able to drive pegs into hard ground. The Jack Wolfskin eVent II was big enough to give me and my kit full shelter. My chair went on the front rack – I was going nowhere without it – and the final major piece of kit was a full-sized track pump. I'd suffered so much with punctures on the last trip because if not getting enough pressure in the tyres so I was taking no chances on this trip. Anyway, speed wasn't of the essence.

With cocky sense of excitement, I passed through security at Terminal 2 in Dublin Airport on 29 May, 2016 to fly to O'Hare Airport, Chicago IL. In 2014, I'd gone through pre-clearance in Dublin and had breezed through domestic arrivals in San Francisco – though Surly had been delivered to International arrivals – and now I would be relaxed flying to O'Hare Airport in Chicago to begin my cycle to the southwest.

I'd booked accommodation for two nights in Hostel International, three blocks south of Adams Street where Route 66 started. It had proven a wise decision in San Francisco – take a day to figure out how to get out of the city, get some last-minute supplies of fuel and food and organise telephone communications.

Most importantly, the Blue Line from O'Hare would bring me to La Salle subway station, just about two blocks from my accommodation in the downtown district. Pre-planning meant that the plan was coming together. In addition to the maps from the Adventure Cycling Association (ACA), I'd gotten a micro-SD card with the United States mapping from eBay for my Garmin eTrex 20. I was ready. Nothing was left to chance. I was even able to tell the baggage handler in Dublin Airport about how Surly had been delivered to the wrong terminal in San Francisco – I could tell from his demeanour that he wasn't really interested in my story.

Everything about the flight was seamless. It arrived on time and the bag containing my panniers was delivered to the right carousel while Surly emerged unscathed from the oversized-luggage belt. I was engaged in conversation by another cyclist as I waited. When I said that it was my intention to cycle Route 66, he asked how I intended to leave the city. He was a local, he said, and wasn't aware of any way to avoid rough areas going south out of town. I didn't have my maps to hand to show him my route and his words lent me a little insecurity. Mick, stay away from negative people!

So far, so good, I thought as I sat on the train bringing me from O'Hare to Chicago city centre. My bike was propped against the window of the bike-friendly carriage and soon I arrived at my station, La Salle. This was the point at which I realised I should have studied the Metro Map more closely. Trying to negotiate an exit from an underground station with steps and no wheelchair access, while accompanied by a reluctant, fully-loaded bicycle is no joke. I was reminded of the old puzzle of the farmer arriving at a river-crossing with a fox, a goose and a bag of corn only to find the boat there would only carry himself and two of the three items. This gave rise to the fox and goose being left together on the bank while the corn was ferried across – in which case the fox would eat the goose, or the goose being left with the corn, in which case the goose would eat the corn. There was a solution to the farmer's conundrum. Anyway, I was reluctant to leave my bags at the bottom while I hauled the bike up. It might be stolen at street level while I went back to retrieve the bags – or the bags might be gone when I got back to them. The only solution was to manhandle the lot together, step by agonising step, to the street. I have a policy of never trying to lift the fully-loaded bicycle, so I have never an idea how much it actually weighs. Boy, were these steps steep! Drag, squeeze the brakes, pause, another step closer to the top! Luckily, a Chicagoan came to my aid near the top – just before my strength gave out – and Surly, with all my bags intact emerged, blinking into the warm Chicago evening.

Hostel International Chicago was only a couple of blocks away along W. Congress Parkway and my booking was acknowledged on arrival. Surly was "housed" in the Luggage store and I made my way to the four-bed dorm on the third floor with the bare minimum of baggage.

Too early for bed, I set off with my Garmin to test out the mapping on the micro-SD card that I'd purchased online. My first attempts to get my location didn't augur well as the map showed Mayo to be over 4,000 kms away and no indication of my current location. This was not the start I was hoping for. At least I had my paper maps and, who knows, I might come across a Garmin store where I might buy a proper card – instead of taking the cheap route of buying one on eBay. I put the Garmin in my pocket and strolled around the area, getting my physical bearings before settling for a beer and a bite to eat.

To my delight, the Garmin realised it was in the US and not in Ireland and the streets of downtown Chicago came alive on the screen. I reset the trip data – which had shown my trip from home – and I was prepared for the off.

I would explore the city tomorrow, as I went in search of my favourite outdoor store, REI, and my supplies of food, fuel and any other knick-knacks that might take my fancy.

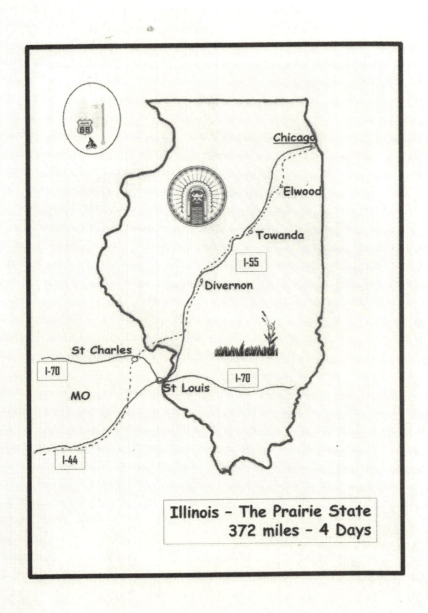

Chapter 2

<u>Illinois – The Prairie State</u>

Day 1 Tue 31 May
Planned: Joliet IL
Actual: Elwood IL
Distance: 125 kms / 78 miles
Total so far: 125 kms / 78 miles
Accommodation: Free in Town Park

Buckingham Fountain near the waterfront, an elaborate landmark dating from 1927, is the accepted starting point for the Adventure Cycling Association route for Route 66. Although the official start point is on Adams St, the difference is negligible and no cyclist wants to become a cropper on the first day. So, at eight o'clock on a nice sunny morning, I crossed from there to the Lakefront Trail set off southwards along Lake Michigan with the opening lines of Bad Bad Leroy Brown echoing in my head.

Well the South side of Chicago
Is the baddest part of town
And if you go down there
You better just beware
Of a man named Leroy Brown.

The cautionary words of the man I'd met at the airport the night before, who couldn't figure a safe way out of the city to the south, gave me cause for concern, but I felt good as I pedalled along this trail. Well-used by commuters, I got any number of friendly waves as I cycled. Words of encouragement were welcome as I headed into the unknown. The trail stretched for eighteen miles and I'd explored a little of it – to the north – the day before. Now I was relaxed, knowing that there was little enough navigation to be done for a while – and no hills for a long time. Now that my Garmin had discovered America, it was about time in the saddle and I had all the hours of the day to move as I pleased, fast or slow.

I made my way south past the Aquarium, Soldiers Field and through Burnham Park, along the shore of Lake Michigan and I felt comfortable in the saddle because I was fitter and better-prepared for the start of the journey than I had been the last time I'd begun on American soil. Anyway, Illinois, the Prairie State, is relatively flat and the first few days would give me a chance to become accustomed to the weight of the gear, while I played around with the balance by moving stuff from pannier to pannier. I felt a little overdressed – and a little self-conscious – with the full-sized pump strapped onto the rear rack. I'd found the REI store at N. Halsted Street and was well-equipped – a few dehydrated meals and fuel for my mini-Trangia, which I hadn't tried out before leaving home. The brand was so reliable that I didn't think it needed verification. Travelling by bike is perfect for limiting purchases. If it needs to be carried, careful consideration must be given to whether or not it's needed. Anyway, the purpose of having dehydrated meals is to ensure they never have to be eaten.

Around Wolf Lake, south of Chicago, I went astray. Normally a bit of a pain, on this occasion it was a stroke of luck as I crossed my first state line, mistakenly entering Indiana. A cyclist, Jerry Carroll, who was happy to stop and chat, put me right. I worked my way around the eastern shore of the lake, along Sheffield Av. where I got on the Burnham Greenway Trail to Calumet City and around Chicago Heights to the Old Plank Road Trail. This 22-mile long paved rail-trail connects the Illinois towns of Chicago Heights, Park Forest, Richton Park, Matteson, Frankfort, New Lenox and Joliet. It was too early to stop in Joliet and I'd missed the campsite on the

Chicago side of town, so I continued on along Washington St which became, finally, Historic Route 66. I was on my way.

In early America there were only two ways to get around, by water or by trail. Most roads were unimproved and many followed trails used by the Native Americans. There were few bridges and weather often made passage on land difficult. Water transport facilitated carriage of greater volumes but destinations were limited to places on navigable waterways. Before being converted to a rail-trail, the Old Plank Road Trail HAD played a major role in the early transportation history of Illinois. For years it had been a trail used by travellers on foot or on horseback and while it took six years to build a railway on the route, it took twenty years to dismantle the same railway, as conflicting opinions raged over its post-rail use. Citizens agitated against the trail with legislators in Springfield. The townships had public meetings to involve the public on decisions about its use and some people hated the trail, believing that people would come into the neighbourhood, steal things out of their homes, and go down the trail to make their escape. As opposition to the idea of a recreational trail grew, supporters of the decided to organise. The Sierra Club, local conservation groups, and The Nature Conservancy became more involved. A special support group called the "Old Plank Road Trail Association" was formed to raise public awareness, publish a newsletter and organize special events. Finally, in July 1997 the trail was opened for use and it became a recreational trail, a nature preserve corridor, a green belt and an alternative transportation network.

I was intrigued by the opposition to the trail because it seems to mirror the objections of residents to the east of Galway City in Ireland who recently objected to a similar bicycle way through their area because it might provide an avenue of escape for thieves. When I stayed at the firehouse in Utica in Kentucky in 2014, I was most surprised by the vision of the Volunteer Fire Department there. Dan, the Fire Chief had explained that they'd integrated into the planning of the new building, the ability to host cycle-tourists and hikers as they passed through. I was amazed that everything was open – that all the equipment would be totally accessible – and asked if they weren't concerned that something might be stolen. Dan figured that cyclists were more likely to leave stuff than take stuff. It's a pity that it seems that, twenty years on, communities in an urban area of the West of Ireland are voicing concerns that were seen to be unfounded in both urban and rural United States.

From the perspective of a stranger cycling in at six in the evening, Elwood is a small place with little going for it. The map indicated a place to eat, but I must have missed it. Perhaps I skirted the main town area. An explosion at the Joliet Ammunition Plant anti-tank mine fuse assembly building on June 5, 1942, killing forty-two average-guy workers, is commemorated by a bronze man carrying a lunch box, located across the street from the entrance to the Abraham Lincoln National Cemetery where the eligibility criteria for burial is very clear according to the website – "Burial in a national cemetery is open to all members of the armed forces who have met a minimum active duty service requirement and were discharged under conditions other than dishonourable. A Veteran's spouse, widow or widower, minor dependent children, and under certain conditions, unmarried adult children with disabilities may also be eligible for burial. Eligible spouses and children may be buried even if they pre-decease the Veteran. Members of the reserve components of the armed forces who die while on active duty or who die while on training duty, or were eligible for retired pay, may also be eligible for burial."

President Lincoln's legacy is especially important to the people of Illinois, where he worked and lived. He is remembered for his successful law practice and elected service as a resident of Illinois. An Illinois State Assemblyman and an Illinois Representative, prior to his election as President of the United States, he is buried in the Oak Ridge Cemetery near the State Capital in Springfield, IL. Cemeteries – particularly military cemeteries – are normally an attraction for me but now I was concerned with finishing for the day. Somewhere to put down roots for the night needed to be found and Elwood wasn't exactly buzzing with activity, so I continued along West Mississippi Av until O'Connor Park appeared on the left. The pavilion was already occupied so I swung over. I'd done enough for the first day – and there was a threat of imminent rain.

Jakob, a bike traveller and sole occupant of the park pavilion, was from Berlin, Germany, and had already been a month on the road. He had cycled from New York and was mainly trying to use Warmshowers hosts and a bit of couchsurfing. I was under no illusion about his pace. He was less than half my age and probably no more than two-thirds of my weight! Like me, he had just left Chicago and was bound for LA eventually – though he was vague about exactly when he hoped to reach the west coast. I was unlikely to have found a cycling partner, because I like predictability about movement if not destination. Jakob seemed to have no certainty – or plan.

I'd been lucky with the first day. The ground had been mainly flat and I'd found shelter. I'd stayed mainly dry through two thunderstorms and, although the evening sky was darkening ominously, I was under cover for the night. Preparing my food, I managed to burn my hand. It seemed that the clean fuel I'd bought in the REI store was for a MSR cooker and not for a Trangia. It's not good to get too close to petrol with a lighter. Luckily the Trangia cooker survived – though the rubber seal around the cap was now a memory. I took at least one layer of skin off the base of my thumb and didn't know if I was supposed to keep the air away from it or expose it. I couldn't be bothered Googling it.

The trouble with the ACA maps is that they rarely let a person see what's off the route. In the case of Elwood, I would have been totally oblivious to the fact that this was one huge Intermodal site with a major

Exxonmobil Corporation site, a Walmart distribution site and the BNSF Logistics Park for Chicago. I would become well-acquainted with the Burlington Northern Santa Fe Railway over the coming weeks, but for now, I just unrolled my sleeping bag and kip mat and climbed on a picnic table to sleep.

Day 2 Wed 01 June
Planned: Pontiac IL 91 km / 57 miles
Actual: Towanda IL
Distance: 128 kms / 80 miles
Total so far: 253 kms / 158 miles

Accommodation: Free in Town Park

Last time out, my schedule had slipped dramatically in the first days as lack of fitness, lack of preparedness and sudden elevation conspired against me. Now I was faced with a different kind of problem – that of going faster than I'd expected. I was reluctant to find difficulty with this because I didn't know when the speed might drop. Anyway, it was only Day 2!

Rain of biblical proportions had fallen through the night and dawn only exposed the dark and menacing sky. There were positives in the situation in which I found myself. I didn't have to pack a wet tent since the pavilion had provided shelter from the elements. I wasn't familiar with weather patterns and it looked, initially, like this rain could last for the day – in which case I'd be a day behind. That's why the extra mileage on any given day was a bonus.

The gateway to the Walmart distribution centre we could see from O'Connor Park only admitted cars, so the working end of the place must have opened onto Hwy 53. No doubt the inhabitants of Elwood wouldn't have been too happy with a multitude of trucks passing through its streets. On the other hand, the Walmart presence seemed so big that it must almost 'own' the town. Maybe O'Connor Park was built at the same time as the distribution centre – as a gift?

Gemini Man, Wilmington IL

The rain eased about seven-thirty and I was hungry. Ideally, I liked to get twenty miles under my belt before stopping for breakfast and Pontiac was 42 miles while Lexington was 64 miles down the road. Wrapped up against the mist, I set off at eight. I thought waterproofs might be the order of the day and I even considered riding in sandals to keep my shoes dry.

I rolled into Wilmington, under the watchful eye of its most photographed "citizen", the 'Gemini Giant', a famous landmark on Route 66. During the sixties, these large fibreglass figures could be seen all over America. Called Muffler Men, they were advertising props, holding all manner of tools, from exhausts to hot dogs. As America began to move faster and faster most of these very tall men disappeared. But here in Wilmington, the large green man hangs tight, along with several other historic icons of the past. He is the Gemini Giant, sporting a rocket ship, a remnant of our fascination with outer space.

Wilmington responded to Route 66 with services for the many travellers of the Mother Road. The Eagle Hotel, one of the first buildings erected in the town, in the spring of 1836 and later used as part of the Underground Railroad – a route used to smuggle slaves of the south to freedom in the north – in the days before the Civil War, now served those travelling on the new trail to the west. The Dairy Delight opened in the late 1950s by John and Betty Korelc at 810 E. Baltimore St. In 1965, they expanded the business and renamed it the Launching Pad. The owners saw one of the famous Muffler Men during a restaurant convention. John put one out front, giving it his own twist by making it look like an astronaut and named it the "Gemini Giant", after the Gemini space program. This icon would become one of the most photographed on the Mother Road, and, along with the restaurant, was inducted into the Illinois Route 66 Hall of Fame in 2000. Unfortunately, the business closed for good in 2013.

For me, Wilmington is famous for having an ACE Hardware store. Since leaving Elwood, my mind had been focused on finding fuel for my cooker. I have always found that, in the absence of serious worries, minor issues gain traction. At a tyre shop, I asked and was directed to the store, just off-route.

Replenished, I set off across the Kankakee River and into the Wilmington Shrub Prairie Reserve, heading for Braidwood and the other forgettable towns of Braceville, Gardner, Dwight and Odell, before arriving in Pontiac. I was, finally, along Historic Route 66, travelling beside the Interstate which had replaced the Mother Road and which bypassed all the towns along the way. Every now and then, a sign on the Interstate indicated mileages to the next "Travel Centre". These are effectively motorway service stops. For the long-distance drivers, they have showers and rest areas. For the cyclists, they provide toilet facilities, food and an opportunity to replenish water bottles with lots of ice at the soda fountains of fast-food outlets.

In Odell, a group of Seniors on motorbikes, riding some of Route 66 as part of their late-life crisis, they said, pulled over for a chat. They were obviously unaccustomed to seeing seniors on bicycles, but, I suppose those cyclists who burden themselves with all the necessities of survival and head off unsupported are very much a subset of cyclists with whom those on motorbikes would have little in common. We chatted for a while and parted. I met them again on the outskirts of Pontiac – at the Old Log Cabin restaurant – where they said the chicken was fantastic. That recommendation was good enough for me and, anyway, it was past my lunchtime. I had to agree with their verdict. Built in 1926, the restaurant originally faced the older Route 66 alignment. It is said to have been lifted and turned 180 degrees when the alignment changed at the intersection of Pontiac Road (two-lane 66) and the four-lane 66 on the north edge of town. The building has been expanded over the years and is a classic example of the economic significance that Route 66 had on roadside businesses. Its tourist value now demonstrates the need for re-invention from time to time.

In Pontiac, Will, a local, became my self-appointed guide, bringing me through The Route 66 Association of Illinois Hall of Fame and Museum which features thousands of artefacts and memorabilia related to Route 66 – The Mother Road. He explained the Route 66 connection and the transport issues of the route. The car was king – there wasn't a lot given over to bicycles. I didn't want to occupy his time, but he said he loved meeting people and, anyway, the crops were planted on his farm and it gave him the opportunity to goof off. I passed a very pleasant hour chatting with him and the volunteers manning the exhibits. They were delighted at a cyclist stopping off – they normally got bikers in leathers! On the outskirts of town a silhouette metal sculpture caught my eye. It was outside the Police District 6 Headquarters and was a figure of a trooper astride a motorbike. The information said that The Illinois State Police (ISP) was formed in 1922 to protect motorists. Twenty officers patrolled the state on surplus World War I Harley-Davidson motorcycles. Radio-equipped cycles revolutionized communications in the 1930s. The ISP shifted toward squad cars and ended motorcycle patrol in 1949.

Too early to consider stopping, I headed on and, because of the heat, was sorely tempted by the municipal swimming pool in Chenoa, where I chatted with a few local college kids on summer break. I settled for a soda and refilled water bottles before continuing to Lexington where I made the further decision to avoid paying for a motel. I would continue on to Towanda – population of less than five hundred with a filling station and a library. That would do for the night. Any further and I was in Bloomington and I was aware, from experience, that smaller communities are more welcoming than the bigger towns.

So that was how I came to be sitting in the scruffy bandstand of the dusty and unused excuse for a town park, a green patch of ground behind some dubious-looking accommodation that had definitely seen better days. If this had been in a more urban setting, I'd have passed on the opportunity to stay – even if was free of charge. There were still a couple of hours to nightfall and I just relaxed, my shirt drying and gathering dust on the balustrade. I was a little unhappy that the volume of passing traffic seemed to indicate I would be more open and observable than I'd hoped and thought that, just maybe, I should have asked at Kicks Bar and Grill on the way into town. There had been a green patch of ground at the back, but at the time I thought to look further ahead.

The traffic continued as the evening went on. It led me to believe that Hely St was some kind of "rat-run" and that might have explained the dusty town park's lack of use. I suppose that, because the town was only nine miles from Bloomington, it was, in reality a suburb and was bound to have evening traffic. A few dog-walkers used the streets but nobody approached me. I settled for the night on a park bench as darkness fell. A police car, lights flashing, responded to a call nearby and I settled down again.

I only became aware that I'd finally fallen asleep when a policeman woke me at one in the morning, with the normal "Are you alright?" question. He'd become aware of my presence when light reflected from my panniers and had come to investigate. Satisfied as to my lack of evil intent, he wished me goodnight and pleasant dreams.

Day 3 Thurs 02 June
Planned: Atlanta IL
Actual: Divernon IL
Distance: 174.3 kms / 108 miles
Total so far: 427.3 kms / 266 miles
Accommodation: Free camping local Sportsmans' Club

At five in the morning, it still wasn't bright enough to get on the road, so I headed to the neighbourhood gas station for a wake-up coffee and a bagel. It was a comfortable 64⁰ F as I headed for Bloomington and on through small towns to Lincoln, stopping for a coffee in McDonald's in McClean where I was immediately given a "senior" cup for seventy-four cents. Happy Days!

As the heat of the day kicked in, I was happy to stop at small local places for coffees or sodas. Peggy's Place was a small bakery in Lincoln and did a lovely lemon pie. The Wild Hare Café in Elkhart, a further fifteen miles along the road provided a lunch of a chicken salad sandwich with a mushroom and wild rice soup. It was a wonderful restoration of my dignity. My dining in these establishments was evidence that I wasn't on the same budget as many touring cyclists who pride themselves on spending as little as possible. I have always felt it necessary to contribute to the local economy rather that to the multi-national gas stations.

I lost some miles in Springfield looking for a campsite that didn't materialise, but it gave me the opportunity to get a feel for the Land of Lincoln. History came alive around every corner. The city is home to more Lincoln sites than anywhere else in the nation, from Abe's house and law offices to his presidential museum. Route 66 was represented by plenty of Americana in the form of classic diners and roadside attractions. The Interurban Trail brought me across Lake Springfield on a great cycleway – a much-used recreational amenity – and into Chatham, where I dropped into the local firehouse to get my water bottles refilled. The fireman on duty gave me directions to get me back on the right road for Divernon, because it required a number of country lanes to get round the Interstate that was becoming my constant companion. I was even becoming accustomed to the traffic noise and I was fine as long as there were frontage roads to ride on – otherwise I'd have to take my chances on the shoulder.

To confirm the route, I pulled up outside a house on the road. James, with his son, Stephen, offered me water. I said I'd enough, but when he offered a beer, I gratefully accepted, saying that it wasn't long to day's end. I'd looked gift horses too often in the past, so I rested up for thirty minutes chatting as they asked me about my trip and about Ireland. I only had another twelve miles to cover.

The Corner Bar in Divernon was a welcome stop and, leaning the bike against the wall, I looked forward to sitting at a bar counter with a beer. This time round, I wasn't actively chasing craft beers – I was just happy to have a cold one. The front wheel of the bike had begun to emit ominous noises and I worried that I might have to find a bike shop in the very near future. I'd check it later. As I sat at the counter, the other four patrons and the girl inside the bar lit cigarettes. I remarked that, in Ireland, we were no longer allowed that luxury. The barmaid, Elise, said that the same applied here and if it offended me, they would stop. No problem for me, especially as she had just made a phone call that secured me permission to camp in the Sportsmans' Club, just outside town.

This was as good an excuse as any to have a second beer while she filled me in on the town. It was named after Diana Vernon, a character in the Walter Scott novel, Rob Roy. Apparently, the landowner who established the town in the late 1800s was quite taken with the book. The population is about eleven hundred and dropping. The rail line passes through – but doesn't stop. The town's only other claim to fame, she said, is that the biggest lump of coal mined in the United States, and currently housed in the Museum of Science and Industry in Chicago, came from Divernon. Fascinating and all as this nugget of information was, I was starving and took my leave, thanking them for securing my campsite. At the end of the square was Patsy's on the Square, where I pigged out on the "Over the Top" Burger and fries – and it was!

My sleeping quarters for the night were shared with the frogs on the lake. They were active and vocal. My tent was deployed for the first time and I slept badly in the humidity. Still, nothing was likely to disturb me here – it only got used at weekends for fishing and shooting.

Day 4 Fri 03 Jun
Divernon IL to St Charles MO
Distance 166.1 km/ 103.7miles
Total so Far 593km / 372 miles
Accommodation: House Guest

The dew-drenched tent was packed at five forty-five and I got on the road at six. Elise, from the Corner Bar had said that the owner was in the habit of coming in early and that there would undoubtedly be a cup of coffee going if I stopped off on my way out of town. Unfortunately, either I'd started too early or the boss had overslept, but there wasn't a sign of life as I cycled past. Still, the good news was that I'd discovered that the noise from the front wheel was only a minor detail – the calliper brakes weren't releasing completely and were rubbing on the rim. I could breathe a sigh of relief as all I'd have to do was reach forward and tug at them.

I continued south on the frontage road of Interstate 55 in the direction of St Louis. I was already a day ahead and my schedule was gone out the window. I would leave the route briefly to visit with Richard Tadlock and his wife, Maria. I'd met Richard near St Charles, on the banks of the Missouri River as I came to the end of the Katy Trail in 2014. He had, when he'd heard of my plan to cycle Route 66, invited me to stay a night with him. This would be a chance to revisit a lovely spot in the centre of the US and it would connect the two trips nicely. Because it was just northwest of St Louis, I'd be able to skirt the city to the west to get back on the route near Eureka, from where I'd travel alongside the I-44.

I met Charles Dees on the road, south of Farmersville. I could see him cycling on a frontage road on the opposite side of the interstate and I didn't think I was going to cross, but when my frontage road ran out at an overpass, we ended up on the same side. I was delighted to stop, already feeling starved of company. He'd set up camp at one of the rest areas and was cycling up and down along Route 66 getting people's stories as they pedalled the route. I'm not sure if he was ever likely to publish them, but it was a wonderful reason to hang out in the area. The day had dried up nicely and I was in no rush. Illinois is prairie land and flat, so moving forward required little effort. Not only that, but this stretch of road was straight and stopping to chat broke the monotony. We pedalled together as far as Litchfield and had a coffee after I'd visited Walmart for some supplies. This was my opportunity to get back to normal dining off the bike – Idahoan mashed potatoes and Campbell's cans.

I said goodbye to Charles and we parted and he resumed his patrol of this stretch of Route 66 while I headed for Hamel, where I would cut west to Alton crossing the Mississippi and on to St Charles on the Missouri. This was fifty miles from Alton, a bit more of a journey than I'd bargained for – and one I wasn't aware of until I crossed the big river.

I turned onto Hwy 94 at West Alton and travelling between the two great rivers, I could see evidence of flooding, which, to me, looked like an occupational hazard hereabouts. Three men, seated on the verandah of a property, were having an end-of-day beer and I asked if I might fill a water bottle. The younger man said, initially that they had none, but an older one – maybe his father – told him to take me next door to another raised structure. When I asked, the young man said they were only getting back on their feet after being totally flooded out. He filled my water bottles from a water cooler and I realised that they had no running water – or, at least, no drinking water. I thanked the men and apologised for intruding on their evening. The men were sceptical of my reaching St Charles, but I knew that I had no option. There was no campsite between here and there.

The road was quieter than I would have expected and I made good time across the flat agricultural land. If I didn't know better, I'd never have thought that I was just north of a major city. St Louis was only over the horizon, so to speak. I didn't know what was to the east of St Charles, but had I only known that the Katy Trail extended all the way to Machens, I would have had a traffic-free trip right to the Bike Stop Café where I would contact Richard by Facebook. A map would have been handy. I wouldn't have had to face the hill into St Charles that was the final kicker. I was glad to sit with a beer and make contact. Richard arrived to collect me and the bike and brought me to his home, where he introduced me to his wife, Maria. I had a wonderful evening in their company. A shower, laundry and pizza, with chat until I began to lose focus about nine o'clock. It had been a one-hundred mile day and I was ready for the cool sheets provided by a wonderful host.

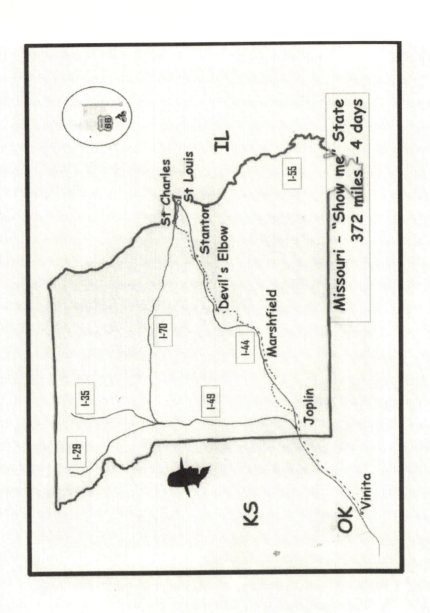

Chapter 3

Missouri – "Show Me State"

Day 5 Sat 04 Jun
St Charles MO to Stanton MO
Distance 111 km / 70 miles
Total so Far 704 km / 442 miles
Accommodation KOA $28.75

Charles dropped me to the Trailhead by the river and, with goodbyes and "thank you's", I headed off in the pleasant temperatures. I was rested, well-fed and clean – all pre-requisites for feeling good. The Garmin brought me to Ellisville MO and back on Route 66. Without a large-scale map to keep me aware of my surroundings, I had to pick a point of intersection between where I was and the Route and hope the Garmin brought me there, while avoiding major roads. Luckily, roads in the western suburbs of St Louis are relatively cycle-friendly and I got to a McDonalds for a burrito. I wasn't taking on a great distance so I delayed my onward departure.

Beyond Ellisville, the ACA map sent me along Alt Road to get me off Hwy 109. This involved an hour of sustained climbing – and two minutes of panic – when a dog attacked – before I had a hairy descent at 55kph where I parted company with my speedometer. I wasn't going back up the hill to look for it. The Garmin would, for the rest of the trip, provide that information.

Eureka was my introduction to Interstate 44. This was one of five interstates built to replace the old route US 66 and was upgraded from a two-lane to a four-lane highway between 1949 and 1955 It was going to be my "handrail" from St Louis to Oklahoma City. The Route 66 State Park in Eureka wasn't enough to drag me off route. The website showed it to be an opportunity for non-travellers to feel they knew what Route 66 was. So I kept going west and across the interstate I could see the billboards advertising the Six Flags St Louis Roller Coaster Park. Day tickets start at $64.00. Who'd mind Surly? At least that was my excuse. I didn't need to put my heart under pressure with the rides as described on its website.

Between Gray Summit and St Clair, I felt at home with the surface. It was like an Irish country road. Leafy and shaded, there wasn't a level inch. It was either an uphill crawl or a "hang-onto-your-hat" downhill. None of the hills were overly testing but there was enough to distract from the pleasant surroundings. I was also introduced to trailer parks – with seductive names like Paradise and Sleepy Hollow. Confederate flags flew from the smaller properties along the road and trucks were the vehicles of choice. I would be hard not to generalise, because other than described, I saw nothing to help me form an alternative opinion.

At St Clair, I crossed I-44 to the frontage road and the calm of the country roads was gone. For the next ten miles to my stop for the day, I was kept company by the incessant traffic as it kept the US alive. Steinbeck coined the term Mother Road for Route 66 and it was also known as Main Street USA. The latter name was very appropriate as I watched the trucks going by – a glossary of US advertising. From big semis to RVs and cars, America seemed to be on the move. U-Haul trucks of varying sizes brought my mind back to Larry and Donna, a couple I'd met in the campsite in Bardstown KY in 2014. They'd had to leave rented accommodation – their landlord a victim of the recession. They'd been collateral damage, left homeless and in possession of a rented U-haul truck containing everything they owned – and their dog, who didn't understand the worry of homelessness and who thought they were just on holiday. I could imagine that these trucks, big and small, were all bringing families to a better life. I was being overly sunny in my thinking – real life isn't necessarily like that!

Billboards, extolling the attractions of Jesse James' hideout in the Meramec Caverns became more frequent, so much so that, by the time I got to Stanton MO, I definitely going to visit. I chose the Kampgrounds of America (KOA) campsite as my stop for the day and checked in. When I indicated my intention to visit the caverns, the man on duty said I'd be taking my life in my hands cycling the three miles each way. Drivers, he said, were crazy and if they didn't get me on the way there, they'd get me coming back. I decided that Jesse is giving more to the area now than he ever gave in his lifetime, but that I could forego the experience.

Before the ethnic cleansing

When my pitch was indicated to me, I set up home and headed for the showers. On the way back, I treated myself to a six-pack of beer. I'd have preferred just two bottles, but the store didn't sell singles. I wasn't going to carry the beers with me the following day so I just relaxed and cracked one open, and was chilling out when the campsite manager approached, all apologetic, saying that the folks in the cabin beside my pitch had complained that I was too close to them and asked if I wouldn't mind moving. I said that I had no difficulty with them being too close to me, but I understood that moving their cabin might be more difficult so I'd move. I couldn't see what the problem had been – I mean, I hadn't even begun playing the tin whistle.

With the tent moved outside the exclusion zone, I relaxed again. The guy in the cabin approached me and offered a beer as a peace offering. He said his wife had had a problem and he was sorry I'd had to move. I said that it wasn't any big deal and declined the beer. He left and I ate a dinner of noodles and mash washed down with Bud Light. Not surprisingly, I felt unwell, but it was another day down.

Day 6 Sun 05 Jun
Stanton MO to Devil's Bend MO
Distance 114.6 km / 72 miles
Total so Far 818.6 km / 514 miles
Accommodation: House Guest

Got on the road at seven and was immediately back into the hills. These were the Ozarks, the mountains I'd avoided in 2014 by going north to the Katy Trail. I was just going to have to suck up this punishment for a few days so I looked at the map and picked bite-sized chunks of the day's distance. Sullivan and Bourbon were small communities on the way to my breakfast stop in Cuba. They were quiet on this Sunday morning and traffic was light. At a family diner, my first on Route 66, I had sausage, biscuits and gravy with copious cups of coffee. It tasted a lot better than it looked. A girl, making a takeaway purchase, chatted while she waited for her order. Her husband was in the military locally. She asked about my impressions of her town and I said that I was surprised that, as the US had managed to change French Fries to Freedom Fries, they had kept the name Cuba on the town. She laughed and said, you can never tell how governments think!

I left Cuba behind and headed on. I was glad of the limited interaction. Any conversation which went beyond "please", "thank you" and "have a nice day" was to be welcomed, savoured and prolonged. A few miles further, in Fanning, the sight of the Red Rocker, said to be the world's biggest rocking chair, took my mind off the conversation. I didn't get close to it because there were people hanging around it and, anyway, it wasn't as if I would see more by going up close and personal. It was massive and I wondered why someone would make one that big – but then I remembered that men from my home town in Clonakilty in Ireland had, over successive Christmases, broken the world record for time spent on a see-saw and on a swing-boat. Whatever floats your boat!

The Big Red Chair

Between Cuba and Rolla, a group of cyclists, taking part in a club cycle race, had a start-finish line in a gap on the side of the road. Always glad to meet those who might understand what I was up to, I turned in for a chat. They were very welcoming, offering me fresh fruit for the thirst and then insisted on praying with me for the success of my journey. There was such a crowd laying hands on my bike that I'd have to be safe at least until Oklahoma, from storms, wildfires and bad winds – of the external type!

My breakfast sustained me for the twenty-three miles to Rolla and I was drawn to Panera Bread, a bakery/café chain with free WiFi, where I had a lovely salad sandwich with soup. It's important to eat well at least once a day, I convinced myself. With a population of almost twenty thousand and home to the Missouri University of Science and Technology, Rolla was a bustling spot and I was glad to get off the bike for a while to observe life going past. I relaxed and drank refills of iced water, a luxury that I felt was healthy.

I try to cover two-thirds of my daily distance before lunch so that I can take my time in the latter part of the day when the heat can be energy-sapping. I was still in uphill-downhill mode when I came to the small community of Dolittle. I could see immediately where its name came from. It was the first bit of level ground I'd encountered since I'd left Stanton in the morning. Between Newburg and Waynesville, Route 66 took a little turn at a place called Devils Elbow. Because the map showed a supermarket there – and the turn on the road didn't look normal, I thought it worth checking out.

The Elbow Inn Bar and BBQ was the only building at the side of the road. The outside was crowded with motorbikes and I found a spot to park Surly. This place looked authentic, in the way that Middlegate Station NV had been. A gate opened into a yard where there were picnic tables. I asked a couple if they wouldn't mind me sharing their space and they were welcoming. I got a beer and joined them. Tom, a retired Sgt Maj and Paula, his wife, were bikers who rode with a Retired Combat Vets Association. We chatted and Tom said he'd relatives in Ireland – in Shannon and Belfast. Tom had significant overseas service and was now training to become a policeman in civilian life. Paula was the chatty one while Tom was more reflective – a Texan and proud of it! My resolve to go further drained away when they bought me a beer so I asked at the bar if they would have any objection to my pitching my tent by the river. That was that for the day.

Paula and Tom – bikers and wonderful hosts

I brought a couple of beers back for Tom and Paula and told them I was staying put. They said they'd been talking while I'd been at the bar and they'd like me to come home with them for the night. They'd go home on their bikes and Tom would come back with the truck and collect me and the bike. I thanked them and said I'd be delighted to accept their kind offer.

Two hours later, I was showered and changed and eating pork, rice and greens, beautifully cooked. Tom showed me around the property and we talked about military service and overseas. Before I knew it, I was flagging and it was time for bed. It hadn't been a huge day, but meeting Tom and Paula was memorable. It's these encounters that make the trip really enjoyable.

Day 7 Mon 06 Jun
Waynesville MO to Marshfield MO
Distance 122 km / 76.5 miles
Total so Far 940.6 km / 590.5
Accommodation: $12.00 RV Park

On his way to work, Tom very kindly dropped me off at the top of a hill near Waynesville and I pedalled off about seven-fifteen. I'd only gone a few miles – as far as Hazelgreen – when the map and road works conspired to put me on the Interstate. I wasn't either ready or that desperate so I looked for a route using the Garmin. Down a dirt road that seemed to be getting worse by the metre, I began to understand one of the basic rules of bike touring "If you think you're lost, go on further – just to make sure! Eventually, I came out on an asphalt road and met a lady who, despite living in the area, was equally uncertain as to where the road led. I expected to see a sign, saying "there be dragons that way". Garmin gave me a degree of comfort as it seemed not to backtracking on itself and promised to spit me out in Lebanon, a town of almost fifteen thousand.

About ten miles from Lebanon, I came across Cow Patty's Café and I was well ready for my breakfast. Two pancakes, two fried eggs, and sausage, washed down with coffee and refills of iced water did the trick and the three ladies who ran the joint were very solicitous. They remarked that they'd not had many cyclists even though they were on the edge of the Mark Twain National Forest, from which I'd just emerged. I said that my trip through there was purely a matter of luck but that it had been my good fortune – traffic-free and shaded by large trees. They said that back in the woods was Fort Leonard Wood military base, commanded by a two-star general and the café gets custom from there. I hadn't seen any signs of military life – but then, maybe it was a training area for snipers, in which case, not being seen would be a good thing!

I met "Jackie" from Japan on the road. He was going east and, like me, carried a full-size pump on the rear rack. I no longer felt conspicuous! I was the cyclist he'd come across for a week. His limited English and my non-existent Japanese, made for a very brief conversation and, with handshake from me and bows from him, we wished each other good luck and goodbye. I'm sure he was as wishful for a Japanese-speaker as I was for an English-speaker.

I persevered with the rolling hills for the thirty-three miles through Philipsburg, Conway and Niangua to Marshfield. This, I thought would be a place likely to yield company as it's on the ACA TransAmerican Route. I was wrong. There was little or nothing in the place and the local park had a sign expressly forbidding trespassing between 22.00hrs and 05.00hrs. It's one thing to trespass where I knew I shouldn't be if there's no sign. It's quite another to ignore the sign. I went for dinner in Sheila's restaurant while planning a course of action. One thing was for sure – I wasn't interested in going any further.

At the checkout, I asked if there was a hotel in town and I was directed towards the Holiday Inn Express beside McDonalds. Without giving the price any consideration, I set off and then, beside the hotel – and part of it – was an RV Park, I decided to try my luck. Yes, they did take tents – and the price for me on my own was $12.00. Happy days!

I had a few high points today – and it's always good to note the good points for future reference when the going gets tough and I begin to question myself:

Tom dropping me off at the top of a hill put me in good humour from the start. Coming across Cow Patty's in time for a late breakfast, the conversation made me feel less alone in the world. Meeting Jackie – or whatever his name was - from Japan, convinced me that I wasn't the only cyclist in SW Missouri. Finding the RV Park in Marshfield was good – and rescued this town from being a miserable spot. Finally, the scent of honeysuckle all along the road through the Mark Twain Forest had been a wonderful accompaniment to the shaded pedalling at the beginning of the day.

I was irritated by the No Trespassing sign in the Marshfield Park, and the fact that there was nothing on the ACA map to indicate the RV Park in Marshfield. I was surprised there were no cyclists on the road on the TransAm because this was about the right time of the year for heavy traffic.

I relaxed after my shower and planned the next day – as in I took a brief look at the maps while checking out the options for breakfast – McDonalds, Sonic, Grillo or Subway. Anything would do apart from Taco Bell. I still remember – and not in a good way – mixing that establishment's fare with cycling!

Day 8 Tue 07 Jun
Marshfield MO to Carthage MO
Distance 159 km / 99.5 miles
Total so Far 1099.6 km / 690 miles
Accommodation $51.00 Guest Motel

The hills seemed always to be in my favour and it was a great day's spinning. Breakfast in McDonalds before I fully packed up in the RV Park, set me up nicely. The free WiFi gave me a chance to Skype home and I set off quite happily. Route 66 today had elements of interest which made me think this was why I came on the route. Roadside attractions were preserved, colourful and – in most cases – open. I breezed along at about twelve miles per hour for most of the day and I arrived into Carthage with every intention of doing the other twenty miles to Joplin. However, the traffic on US 96 had shown me why the ACA maps had rerouted cyclists onto the more minor roads north of the real route. Hwy 96 had a miserable shoulder and, even worse, had rumble strips inside the cyclists' territory.

Springfield MO was the big town on the day's ride. It seemed clean and tidy, though it was early when I passed through. The relocation love-bombing website said the "Living in Springfield is easy. It's a place that has everything you need. We have a plentiful and growing job market, great schools, world-class healthcare, and all the entertainment and cultural options of a big city – but with far less stress and an abundance of character and friendliness. All at the same time, you can fast-track your career, afford the home you've always wanted, simplify your commute, and enrich your life amid our natural Ozarks beauty. See what we have to offer for your lifestyle, then live here, and just breathe." I'd almost be tempted, but I reckon I'd have to be comfortable with firearms in this part of the world and I'd had enough of that.

It had two breweries and a couple of wineries and that was probably why they'd located Missouri State University there – saved the students travelling too far for drink! Too early to sample Mother's Brewing Company offerings, I kept going, enjoying the Bonnie and Clyde murals and the silhouette Route 66 signage through the town.

Heading west from Springfield, MO on old Route 66, the scenic stretch of the Mother Road on the way to Carthage provides, according to the blurb, "numerous peeks at the past along this almost abandoned piece of pavement". Though still populated by large farms and ranches, the old towns along this slice of the highway have long passed their prime, dying off when the "killer", I-44, caused them to be bypassed. It was a case of the killer passing the victim forever. Some of the settlements still have a few people living in them, but almost every one of the dozen or so towns that once thrived here, have long since become ghost towns or don't exist at any more.

Old Route 66 meanders westward out of Springfield on Missouri Highway 266 through rolling hills that are situated along the western edge of the Ozark Plateau. Plano Ghost Town is one casualty of the Interstate that replaced Route 66. It's listed on the map as a ghost town, but, in reality, it's just a few buildings that used to have a number of uses. Today, there only two buildings left that clearly pre-date Route 66. One looks as if it might have survived a number of Missouri's many Civil War battles when this old route was known as the "Wire Road", a strategic path extending from St. Louis to Fort Smith, Arkansas.

I continued over gentle hills before arriving at Halltown, a much-diminished survivor of Route 66, which was founded in the 1870s when George Hall opened one of the first stores in the area. In 1879 the post office was established and named after Mr. Hall. During its heyday, serving Route 66, the town supported almost twenty businesses including three grocery stores, a drugstore, a blacksmith shop, service station, garage, and a variety store. In fact, business was so good during those days that Halltown was known as the "Antique Capital of the World."

Today, Halltown has a bit of small town charm in but, mostly, its boarded up stores are quiet. I stopped at the one store that remains open, the Whitehall Mercantile. There was a treasure trove of antiques and collectibles displayed from floor to ceiling in this long-standing building. First built in 1900 as a grocery and general store, it provided a rich view of the past in both its building and its merchandise. The owner was more interested in chatting than selling. He said that his daughter wasn't going to allow him run the store from next year on, because, she said, it was too much for him. He said he was ninety-four and enjoyed the interaction with people passing through. I bought a few postcards from him and asked where the post office was. "Down the street on the right, opens at noon", he said, "if the young woman who runs it opens up on time. It's the problem with young people these days – you can't depend on them."

I had visions of a flighty young thing whose thoughts might have been more occupied with social life than her work, so it was with some surprise that I turned up to the post office just after midday to find a septuagenarian behind the counter. I had to smile to myself at the man in the mercantile, a great-grandfather full of piss-and-vinegar and how his perception and mine diverged. He came in the door of the post office while I was there and began haranguing the 'young' one inside the counter. She gave as good as she got and it was obvious that they had a great relationship. It was a pleasure to be a small part of life in small-town America.

The 1930 Las Vegas Hotel and Barber Shop, the old Hamilton Brown Shoe Company, and several other old buildings are all boarded up. The population in 2010 was listed as one hundred and seventy three, down sixteen in ten years. It's only a matter of time!

Paris Springs Junction, a few miles down the road took its name from the town of Paris Springs, bypassed by Route 66 in the 1920s. Soon after the road opened, a few businesses set up to take advantage of the many travellers. A dome-shaped cobblestone garage was one of the first buildings to be built at the junction in 1926. Four years later a Sinclair station was built next to the garage. Owned by Gay and Fred Mason, the couple also added a cafe and three cabins to their little enterprise, which they called Gay Parita, after Mrs. Mason. Taking advantage of the busiest road in America, the Masons did a brisk business fixing flat tires, and selling gasoline, sodas and sandwiches for the next twenty-five years. When Gay Mason died in 1953, Fred continued to operate the business, but when tragedy struck again, burning down the Sinclair station in 1955, Fred retired to his home behind the burned out station. He died in 1960.

Gay Parita

When Route 66 was decommissioned, the junction was bypassed by I-44. For several decades, the property sat silent, used only as a residence. However, it was purchased by Gary and Lena Turner who rebuilt the old Sinclair Station, which, today, shining and new, attracts a new generation of Route 66 travellers. While the "new" station isn't an exact replica of its predecessor, its facade is in character for the 1930s era. The "station" doesn't sell anything – no gas, no sundries, no gimmicks or tourist memorabilia – just memories and enthusiasm. Gary Turner passed away in January 2015 and his wife Lena just a few months later. Gary spent many days/years welcoming roadies from all over the world, sharing Route 66 history, and promoting the road. But there is still life at the Gay Parita, as Gary's daughter Barbara took over in 2016. I was a fortunate recipient of Barbara's goodness when I arrived, hot and sweating. A group of people were sitting on the porch, when I stopped to take a picture. I was immediately invited to take a seat and tell them about my journey. They asked if I wanted anything and I said I'd like a bottle of cold water. It was produced immediately and when I went to pay, Barbara said that they weren't a store and that they maintained this structure because it was her parents' dream.

The other grouping comprised two couples, unknown to each other. One was from Melvin, KY and the other was from Jefferson, MO. When I mentioned that I'd passed through both places on my trip across the States in 2014, they were amazed. Not so much the couple from Jefferson because that place is a state capital, sizeable and relatively local, but Melvin is too small to even have its population mentioned in Wikipedia!

The day was pleasant and I could take my time. From here, the ACA maps took me off the main road to avoid the bad traffic conditions and thirty-three perilous miles became fifty-seven carefree miles along country roads – mainly straight with right-angled turns. There was nothing natural about these roads – they didn't follow ancient trails and animal tracks like country roads in Ireland. These were carved from the land, creating sections that carried the unimaginative names of M, UU, N and 110. Still, they brought me to Carthage and the Guest House Motel and public laundry. I'd covered one hundred and fifty-nine kilometres and was half-a-mile short of one hundred miles. I could have ridden around the parking lot a few times to make the clock tick over, but what was the point. I was knackered – in a nice way. The Filipino girl at reception indicated a number of local dining options, Mexican, a burger joint, a pancake house and a bakery – which was probably closed by now. Weighing the options, I came down on the side of proximity, remembering the words of cyclist Seán Kelly, "Never stand when you can sit, never sit when you can lie down and never, ever, walk!" Medina's Taqueria served up a mean burrito and a bottle of Estrella Jalisco. I felt the $51.00 was reasonable value for my night's accommodation with the opportunity to get my laundry done.

Day 9 Wed 08 Jun
Carthage MO to Vinita OK
Distance 136 km / 85 miles
Total so Far 1235 km / 775 miles
Accommodation: $10.00 Park Hill Motel and RV Park

Carthage had more millionaires per capita than any other city in the United States, by the end of the nineteenth century. Wealth derived from the rich deposits of lead and zinc and soon the mine owners began to build fine homes. Huge deposits of gray marble at the north edge of Carthage provided another source of prosperity. The Missouri State Capitol, U.S. Capitol and White House are all faced with marble that came from the Carthage area.

When Route 66 was built through the town, Carthage was proclaimed by its Chamber of Commerce as "The Open Gate to the Ozarks" and, soon, all manner of services began to spring up to serve the travellers on the Mother Road.

At the intersection of Missouri Highway 71 and Route 66, I came across the historic Boots Court Motel. Built as a tourist court in 1939 by Arthur Boots, this popular stop along the old Mother Road, once advertised a radio and every room and reportedly, Clark Gable once stayed in Room 6. Across the road, the Boots Drive-in, now gone, would offer fountain service and "Breakfast at any hour!" Nowadays, these, in Ireland are offered as all-day breakfasts – sustenance for any touring cyclist!. The drive-in thrived throughout the 1940s but declined after the Interstate bypassed Carthage and finally closed in 1971. Today, the building is used as a bank.

Carthage is home to one of the few surviving drive-in theatres left in America. It's apparent that much of the preservation along this stretch of the route has been carried out by real enthusiasts When the Goodman's bought the historic drive-in, it was in a state of much disrepair and they've brought it back to life.

As well as the suburb of Carthage, to get to Joplin, I had to go through other suburbs, Carterville and Webb City. The positive was that built-up areas deliver more choice in the nutrition stakes and this has to be weighed against the greater possibility of encountering drivers of the asshole variety. I had left the motel off without breakfast – it wasn't included – and I took on the traffic of Central Ave., Oak St and Old 66 Boulevard to Carterville. Traffic, at that hour, seemed to be light enough, or maybe the ACA had gotten its act together. Riding down a residential street, a truck came up beside me and the driver lowered his window. I braced myself for a verbal onslaught about taking up his tax-funded road, but he just said there was a very good diner, The Rooster's Crow, at the next junction. I was ready for breakfast and gave him the thumbs-up as he headed on.

I headed there and ordered a sizeable breakfast with coffee. A few minutes later, the man, who obviously worked in a construction-related business, came in with his helper and we got talking. He said he was from the locality and that he'd been coming here for breakfast for over fifty years. He said Carterville was a real community, fiercely proud and hated to be referred to as part of Joplin. He went on his way and I relaxed over my third coffee before asking for the check.

Just as I was readying to leave, a lady came up to me and said that she and her husband had paid for my breakfast. I hadn't even been speaking to them, but she said that they'd seen my bike outside and felt I could do with feeding to pedal that thing.

Joplin MO, was the end of the second map of the ACA Route 66 series. Opening a new map brings an element of excitement. Short of having company, this was as good as it gets. I'd been in Missouri for a number of days now and I was suddenly going to move from what had been the 'Confederate' South to the Yankee North as I moved from Missouri through a small corner of south-eastern Kansas. It was only a few miles but it gave the feeling of distance as I'd pass through Kansas into Oklahoma in the space of a couple of hours.

The city of Joplin, Mo, the self-styled lead mining capital of the world, was first settled by the Reverend Harris G. Joplin in 1839. The minister held church services in his home for other pioneers in the area long before the city of Joplin was ever formed. Lead was discovered in the Joplin Creek Valley before the Civil War, but mining operations were interrupted by the war. In 1870, a large lead strike brought many miners to the area and numerous mining camps were set up. A town sprang up on the east side of the valley and was named for Joplin Creek.

Soon afterwards, a Carthage resident named Patrick Murphy filed another town plan on the west side of the valley, calling it Murphysburg and before long, a fierce rivalry sprang up between the two towns. Before it could get out of hand, the Missouri State General Assembly combined the municipalities in 1873 and today, Murphysburg is a residential historic district of Joplin.

With the influx of miners, Joplin became a wild town, filled with saloons, dance halls, gambling establishments, and brothels – so much so, that press referred to the city as being in the midst of a "Reign of Terror." The riches of the mining fields also drew investors and speculators and a need for a banking institution was obvious. Though Patrick Murphy had lost his bid for the new city of Murphysburg, he saw opportunity and, in 1875, formed the Banking House of Patrick Murphy.

While Joplin was put on the map by lead, it was zinc, often referred to as "jack," that built the town. With the railroads passing through the area, Joplin was on the verge of dramatic growth. What began as a simple mining town was soon filled with smelters, mines, large homes, businesses, and the ever present saloons, the most popular of which, the House of Lords, featured a bar and restaurant on its first floor, gambling on the second, and a brothel on the third floor. The building still stands today.

Joplin was became the centre of the mining activity for the Tri-State Mining District of Missouri, Kansas and Oklahoma by the turn of the century and the city boasted more than twenty-six thousand people. Construction centred around Main Street, with many bars, hotels, and fine homes nearby. Trolley and rail lines made Joplin the hub of southwest Missouri and it soon became the lead and zinc capital of the world.

In 1926, Route 66 made its way through Joplin and all manner of service businesses began to spring up for travellers. Bonnie Parker and Clyde Barrow set up home there for several weeks in 1933, plying their robbery trade at several local businesses. When tipped off by a neighbour, the Joplin Police Department attempted to apprehend the pair at their hideout, but the pair escaped after killing Newton County Constable John Wesley Harryman and Joplin Police Detective Harry McGinnis.

Route 66 created a prosperous environment for Joplin with the extensive traffic generated by Americans finding themselves with more leisure time than ever before after World War II. In the name of progress during the 1960s and 1970s, many of the landmarks were demolished. So, while many historic views still exist, they are so interspersed with modern structures that it doesn't invite stopping the bicycle.

I'd been very conscious of the risk I ran in taking on the bicycle trip at this time of the year. Previous experience had taught me that I'd nothing really to fear from animals or humans. Weather, on the other hand, was very much an unknown and, with the distance and variations in weather between Chicago and the West Coast, I might well experience some difficulty. Leaving Chicago any earlier would have exposed me to significant cold weather in the early days. Any later and the heat in the deserts of New Mexico and Arizona might prove my undoing. Beginning when I did, exposed me to the risk of storms and tornadoes. My route took me through "tornado alley". The area was prone to them and I really didn't want to experience one. On May 6, 1971, Joplin was struck by a severe tornado resulting in one death and 50 injuries, along with major damage to many houses and businesses. Unfortunately, it wouldn't be the last time. On May 22, 2011, the city was struck by an even more devastating tornado, killing at least 158 people, injured 1,150 others and caused damages of $2.8 Billion.

The few miles of Kansas, through which Route 66 passes has been well-preserved and I travelled on a stretch of the original route at Galena. This was instructive as it clearly demonstrated why the road would never have been a hit with leisure cyclists – it was as if it was cobbled and I was glad to get back on a bit of real road and ride the few miles into Baxter Springs. I hadn't signed up to off-road biking.

From its founding, the little township of Baxter Springs had, for several years, made little progress. By 1876, the community's population had fallen to only about eight hundred residents, but, during this period of hard times, someone discovered that the mineral springs had wonderful health-giving properties and Baxter Springs became a famous health spa. A park was laid out on Military Avenue near the bathhouses and people came from across the country to drink the healing waters. A town always needs a miracle!

On April 19, 1876, two members of the James-Younger Gang, Charlie Pitts and Bill Chadwell, rode into town and robbed the Crowell Bank. Though Jesse and Frank James may have been involved in some manner in planning the robbery, they were not seen. Almost three thousand dollars were said to have been taken from the bank. This building now houses the Café on Route 66 with a sign on the side of the building that says it was once robbed by Jesse James. The prices didn't reflect robbery either.

Route 66 provided an additional source of revenue, when it passed through the town, as gas stations, cafes and motor courts sprouted up. In the 1930s, the Baxter Springs General Store was said to have been robbed by Bonnie and Clyde twice within one week. The legend says that they came through Baxter Springs and robbed the store, only to rob it just a week later when they travelled through town again. They, seemed, unlike the myth, to have been quite parochial in their actions.

My coffee stop at the Café on the Route sustained me for my crossing over into my next state of Oklahoma. Kansas has the smallest portion of Route 66 at just over thirteen miles and the state line came almost as a surprise. A succession of small settlements, closely spaced, shortened the journey to Miami and I got there at about half-one, just in time for lunch.

With only about thirty miles to go to Vinita, where I hoped to stop for the day, I was being careful and taking it easy. I took a few drinks stops after lunch at various stores as the temperature headed to the mid-thirties, a noticeable increase since Missouri. In Afton, just fifteen miles from the end, I found a pharmacy where I bought an antiseptic spray and two packets of plasters. The burn on my hand from Day One seemed to have gotten uglier and I wanted to keep it clean.

My concern, when I arrived at the Park Hill Motel and RV Park outside Vinita, was that they might not be bike-friendly, but I needn't have worried. The young man at reception took my ten bucks and showed me to a spot beside the washroom and got me a key to the facilities. My priority was to get the tent pitched, then shower and stomp on my clothes to get the dust out of them. I hung them on a makeshift line with safety pins and then I set about treating my injuries. For a couple of days, I'd been aware of what's called a hot spot caused by the saddle. I treated it with the antiseptic spray, hoping to prevent it turning into what could be a tour-ending saddle sore. Next for attention was my hand. Exposure to the shower had been stinging and it looked bad – it didn't have the redness I'd have associated with healing. So I sprayed it, bandaged it and tried to forget about it while preparing my dinner.

The clientele here was, most definitely, not tourist. I'd brought a copy of John Steinbeck's The Grapes of Wrath with me on this trip and I had wanted to wait until I was at the start of the Joad's journey west, before I started it. This seemed like an opportune time and I opened it to read about Tom Joad's return home from prison and the walk he'd had from the road to his folk's house. I could identify with him taking a rest in the shade of a tree as I'd taken the opportunity on quiet roads the previous day to stretch out on a grassy bank and have an hour's snooze. Here, in this RV Park, were families of migrant workers, living in cheap motel rooms while the wage-earners picked up whatever temporary employment existed. Ragged barefoot children wandered around the area where I camped and a couple of them paused to watch me prepare my dinner of mashed potatoes and Campbell's stew.

I was well ahead of my schedule, expecting to reach this spot four days later than this but, I'd been feeling strong and there had been nothing significant to entice me to avail of the rest days I'd factored into the journey. It had been an ongoing issue for me – and a limitation of solo touring – that being alone didn't create in me any great desire to pause and take in the sights. The sights along Route 66 had been mostly visual landmarks, best viewed through the windshield of a car rather than warranting in-depth exploration. My extra days were a contingency fund if I were to fall victim to unforeseen events – weather, sickness, wildfires or mechanical failure. It was a long way to Los Angeles and I might yet need those days, but I didn't want to arrive at journey's end too early. Doing so would only incur significant accommodation costs.

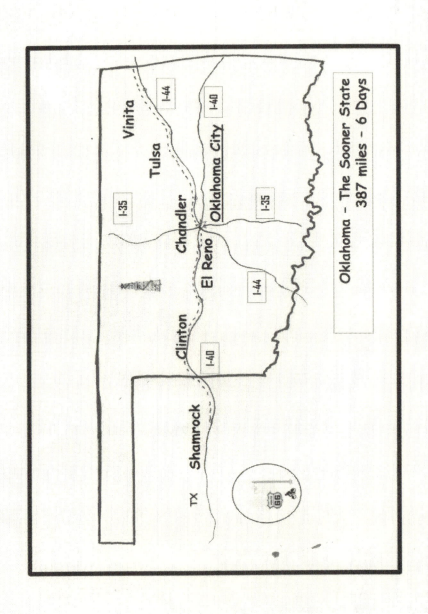

Chapter 4

Oklahoma – The Sooner State

Day 10 Thurs 09 Jun
Vinita OK to Tulsa OK
Distance 112 km / 70 miles
Total so Far 1352 km / 845 miles
Accommodation: Stealth – in College Grounds

The bright light, illuminating the way to the toilets, cast enough light in my direction to make me think it was dawn. This made for a restless night, as from time to time I unzipped the tent only to find it pitch black outside. I was fully intent on getting up at five o'clock, and I dragged myself from the sleeping bag at half-five. The temperatures likely to get to about thirty-seven or thirty-eight degree Celsius as the day went on, so it made sense to get as many miles into the day as possible before three or four o'clock, when the day seemed to be at its hottest.

The large fishing pond on the property of the Park Hill Motel and RV Park had obviously contributed to the heavy dew that meant the tent would be packed wet. The clothes I'd hung out to dry were very damp, but, at least, I'd be cool for a while until the day's heat dried them off so, fuelled by a sachet of oatmeal supplemented with some trail mix, I was on the road before six-thirty. Chelsea, fifteen miles away would make a likely stop for a real breakfast.

Heading west from Vinita, Route 66 winds through several small towns, alternating between two-lane and divided four-lane highway. The old highway still sees regular use among the locals, but some of the communities along this stretch have been left as virtual ghosts, while others are dotted with closed businesses recalling better times. The consistent headwind into which I pedalled, didn't encourage admiration of the scenery. I rolled through White Oak a few miles down the road, but there was very little left in this small town other than a vintage Country Court Motel sign peeking up from the foliage and an old Moose Lodge. Everything else, other than a few homes, has been wiped away by the passing years.

More and more, I had become aware that no community has a divine right of existence. There must be a reason – and when that reason disappears, so will the community. Joplin might have disappeared when the mines closed, but, by then, it had become too big to fail. In 2014, I had cycled through Rico CO, in the Rockies, and found it to be a one-street town. It was hard to believe that in its heyday, it was being considered as the state capital of Colorado. The mines there dried up, the population dropped dramatically and Denver got the honour. There has to be a message, especially for rural Ireland. The amalgamation of farms, the growth of large stores like Tesco, Aldi and Lidl, closure of banks, police stations, post offices and other services have the knock-on effect of causing a drop in population – mainly through migration to more urbanised areas – precipitating further closure of small businesses like pubs, hardware stores and family-run butcher shops, leaving only hairdressers, bookie shops and, perhaps, the odd discount store. A gas station on the edge of town, expanding to provide "better" services to its customers, delivers fast food from its hot and cold deli counter while diners in town can't compete. The downward spiral continues and we finally get a ghost town – except in Ireland, the ones we already have, from the nineteenth century, are referred to as "Deserted Villages" or "Pre-Famine Villages". Ireland is becoming "Americanised".

I was tired from the effort of pedalling by the time I reached Chelsea and I was relieved to prop the bike against the wall of the Main Street Diner, and join the local diners in a mom-and-pop diner. I placed my order and a few minutes later, I heard a voice say, "I'll get that!" Charlie Welch was a member of the Chelsea City Council and he sat with me drinking a coffee while I ate. When he saw that my hand was looking angry and was weeping, he said I should put salt on it to speed up the healing. This was the first person who seemed to know what to do – pharmacists had recommended ointment, sprays and plasters to no avail. In the absence of any better suggestion, I supposed I could do worse than try Charlie's proposed remedy. I nearly screamed as the salt from the table shaker hit the weeping wound. The pain was excruciating and Charlie said I should do it on a daily basis and it would dry up in a matter of days. I wasn't sure if I was prepared for that pain again. I said thanks and goodbye to Charlie, who told me to "be sure and sign the wall!"

Graffiti welcome in Chelsea

Chelsea was first founded in 1870 by a homesick Frisco railroad worker who named the new settlement after his native Chelsea, England. In the beginning, its economic mainstays were cattle and hay, until oil was discovered in 1889. The rich oil, found just west of town prompted the securing a lease from the Cherokee Nation to drill the first oil well in Oklahoma. The oil discovery was responsible, not only for the town's growth, but also for shaping the destiny of the entire state of Oklahoma. Route 66, with its incessant traffic, effectively cut the town in two and an underpass was created to allow pedestrian passage across the road. It was hard to imagine, looking at now, that it was ever needed. In an effort to draw some of the tourist traffic now, the underpass had been cleaned up, painted and reopened as a tourist attraction and visitors were encouraged to sign the walls. I signed and moved on, glad of the break and happy to reflect on the generosity of strangers for the second day in a row.

I was sure that Claremore, the next significant centre of population on the road, would deliver the usual plethora of fast-food outlets with WiFi and air-conditioning. On first viewing, it didn't! Just off Route 66, on Will Rogers Blvd, I came on the Boomerang Diner, which Google says is a "50s-style diner chain for American eats such as burgers & chicken-fried steak, plus breakfast fare." That'd do – there's no point in looking a gift horse in the mouth. It had a soda fountain, air-conditioning, power outlets and big helpings. These are the things that oil the machinery of bike touring.

Claremore got its beginnings when a tribe of Osage Indians arrived, involuntarily, from Missouri in 1802 and established a fur trading post along the Verdigris River. The trading post sat on top of a twenty-five acre mound which came to be known as Clermont, from the French, meaning "Clear Mountain". Over time, traders and Indians alike began to refer to the Chief as "Chief Clermont."

The area became part of the Louisiana Purchase in 1803, and it was designated as Indian Territory. The Cherokee tribe was forced from their eastern homes along the infamous "Trail of Tears" and was given title to the land, including Clermont Mound, without reference to the Osage

Indians who were summarily removed to a reservation, which would later be called Osage County. The Cherokee Indians established its community on Clermont Mound beginning with a general store, a blacksmith shop and a school. In 1874 the post office was established with the intention of naming the town after Chief Clermont. However, due to a clerical error, the name was listed as Claremore, and so it was. The Cherokee, adapted to the "white men's" ways and prospered, organized constitutional governments, published newspapers, and established an extensive educational system. In 1889, when the U.S. Government began to open up unassigned lands in Indian Territory, white men flooded the territory and soon took control of Claremore and, by the turn of the century, Claremore was larger than Tulsa. A test oil well, drilled in Claremore in 1903, failed to deliver oil, but the drillers discovered a large flow of artesian mineral water. Radium bath houses became the rage in Claremore. There didn't seem to be any now – just when I might have done with one.

The Blue Whale

Just east of Catoosa lies the Blue Whale attraction of Route 66. This is an amazing sight and I just had to pull over. Although it was closed, I could appreciate it from the roadside. The brochures said that it is one of the most recognizable icons on Route 66 – and they weren't lying. The attraction was built by Hugh Davis in the early 1970s as an anniversary gift to his wife Zelta, who collected whale figurines. Hugh and Zelta had over forty years of zoological experience when the 80 foot long grinning Blue Whale was built. Hugh was retired by that time, owned the land on which the attraction was built and surprised Zelta with the massive project about which she had no idea, thereby proving beyond reasonable doubt, that the devil makes work for idle hands. Originally, the pond surrounding the massive Blue Whale was spring fed and intended only for family use. However, as many locals began to sneak in to enjoy its cool waters, Davis brought in tons of sand, built picnic tables, hired life guards, and opened his masterpiece to the public.

Originally called Nature's Acres, Davis continued to build the attraction until it eventually included The Fun and Swim Blue Whale and the A.R.K. (Animal Reptile Kingdom). The attraction also featured his brother-in-law, Indian Chief Wolf Robe Hunt, a full blooded Acoma Indian, who was famous, in his own right, for his Indian paintings and as a highly skilled silversmith. Chief Wolf-Robe Hunt once ran the Arrowood Trading post across the highway from the Blue Whale attraction. Soon the pond, giant Blue Whale, and zoo, housed in a wooden ark, attracted both locals and travellers alike. Children flocked to slide down the tail of the large Blue Whale into the cool waters of the pond, as families enjoyed the picnic tables, concessions, and boats provided at Nature's Acres.

The aging couple found that they could no longer handle manage it and, in 1988, the attraction closed. Just two years later, Hugh Davis died and the park fell into disrepair, crumbling from neglect and weather, until, in the early 2000s, a son, Blaine Davis, became a part-time caretaker of his parents' property, and it reopened. A few years later, a large group of volunteers pitched in to help clean the grounds. A local volunteer group, Fins of the Blue Whale, formed in 2009 and began long-term efforts to improve the grounds – including plans to eventually renovate and reopen The A.R.K. as a museum and in the summer of 2011, the Blue Whale was given a fresh coat of paint.

It was probably distraction after the whale attraction that caused me to miss the exit that would have kept me on the Old Route 66. Instead, I found myself on the shoulder of the I-44 with no obvious escape. Then, a bang heralded my first puncture of the trip. I'd done well, getting this far, and, as luck would have it, there was a large Walmart on my right, across a green area. Swearing loudly at the traffic, I hauled the disabled Surly off the interstate, over the wide green area, and into the parking lot for first aid.

This was serious. A bent three-inch nail had skewered the tyre and left me under no illusion about my predicament. The tube would be destroyed. That was of less concern than that the tyre might be holed beyond repair, because, while I carried spare tubes, a spare tyre hadn't figured in my packing list. I had to use a pincers to remove the object and it left a small "bullet hole". I replaced the tube, refitted the tyre and reloaded the bike, before taking a cold drink from the machine conveniently located by the entrance to Walmart. I managed to escape from the parking lot, get under the Interstate and get back on Route 66 on E. 11 Street.

A mile further on, another puncture had me repeating the repair procedure. This was dispiriting in the afternoon heat. I began to believe that the tyre was finished but, without an option, I decided to give it one more chance and headed on again. Perhaps I should have replaced the tyre from the Walmart stock. Worn out, I stopped at a firehouse and asked the fireman on duty if I might fill my water bottles and if they wouldn't mind me putting my chair out front under the tree so I might rest. No problem

– and when I got chatting with him, he said that he was from Chelsea. I mentioned Charlie Welch and his kindness. He knew Charlie and said it was typical of him – a one-man tourist board! My period of relaxation under the tree was rudely interrupted by the presence, in numbers, of ants. They were acrobatic enough to have gained a foothold on my chair before I became aware of them, but I wasted no time in cleaning them off. I took it as a sign that I'd better get back on the road and, with drinks bottles full of iced water, I threw my tired leg over the crossbar and entered into the afternoon traffic to cover the fifteen miles that would get me through Downtown Tulsa and across the Arkansas river. Gene Pitney's 24 Hours from Tulsa was in my head as I jousted with rednecks with loud exhausts on a street that wasn't made for bicycles in the first place.

Catoosa is linked to the Arkansas River system all the way to the Gulf of Mexico and a port, located in a 2,000 acre industrial park and employing more than 2,500 people, offers a year round, ice-free barge service with river flow levels controlled by the U.S. Army Corps of Engineers. The port ships manufactured goods and agricultural products from America's heartland to the rest of the globe.

This bit of information wasn't helping my hunger or my anxiety as I got closer and closer to town. My nerves were frazzled as I passed all the motor dealerships, auto parts shops, used-car lots and auto accessories stores. I felt for the Joad family in their beat-up car making the journey. With the obvious absence of bike shops, I felt as vulnerable to breakdown and mishap as they would have done, but mine was based on non-availability rather than finance. Realising that I hadn't eaten in hours, I pulled off the street to Mimi's Grill. The smallest was a fourteen-inch pizza and I could only get through half of it. I boxed up the remainder to be bungeed to the top of the rear rack. It would do me for breakfast.

Native Americans first settled Tulsa in 1836 when they were forced to relocate along the Trail of Tears. The Creek, Seminole, Lochapoka,

Cherokee, Quapaw, Seneca, Shawnee, and other tribes had to surrender their lands east of the Mississippi River after the passage of the Indian Removal Act in 1830 and each of the larger tribes was given extensive land holdings so they could begin new lives as farmers, trappers, and ranchers. Some called their settlement by the Creek Indian word "Tulsy" which meant "old town." For the next twenty-five years they would lead a peaceful life in a primarily untamed wilderness with only a few white settlers in the area.

When the Civil War broke out, the United States ignored the Indian Territory and sent its troops to war against the Confederate forces. The Creek Indians were torn as to which side to support and many of them believed that they could seek protection to the north in Kansas. However, when they gathered up their families and possessions they were attacked by a force of Texas Cavalry and Confederate Indians northwest of Tulsa where the Cimarron River flows into the Arkansas River and the surviving Union Indians moved into Kansas near the Fort Scott area. Eventually three thousand Creek Indians enlisted, half and half in the Confederate and Union forces. After the end of the Civil War, the Creek Indians returned to their homes in the Tulsa area, where a United States census taken in 1867 showed that the Tulsa area had a population of two hundred and sixty-four Creek Indians. In the aftermath of the Civil War, the Indian Territory, still not subject to any white man's jurisdiction, became an outlaws' refuge. The Indian Territory got a name for being a place where terror reigned and desperadoes thought the laws did not apply to them.

In an effort to tame the wild frontier, President Grant appointed Judge Isaac Parker to rule over the federal district court for the Western District of Arkansas, in Fort Smith, Arkansas. This district had jurisdiction over the Indian Territory and when Parker's tenure began in 1875, he quickly began to enforce the law against the many criminals who had taken over

Oklahoma. His efforts earned him the nick-name of "The Hanging Judge," as order was restored to the area.

More and more white settlers began to move into Indian Territory and, surprise, surprise, the government broke its "permanent" arrangement with the Native Americans. The tribes were forced to accept a number of new treaties which further limited the amount of land each of them held.

The St. Louis and San Francisco Railroad extended its line to Tulsa, in 1882, to serve the cattle business. A stock yard, with cattle-loading pens and chutes, was built near the tracks, and cattle were driven from the Indian Nations and Texas to be shipped to Northern and Eastern markets. The railroad surveyor laid out a number of streets near the railroad tracks. In the beginning, because Tulsa was located in the Creek Nation, it had no legal government or taxes, no public schools, water systems or street regulations, and Tulsa was considered a wide open town. In 1889 the unassigned lands in Indian Territory were opened to white settlers and the flood of people were soon nick-named the "boomers."

Don't frighten the horses

Tulsa changed from a cow-town to a boomtown with the discovery of oil in 1901. A giant oil deposit was found nearby and wildcatters and investors, with their families, flooded into the city of Tulsa. The town spread out in all directions from downtown. Four years later, in 1905, a new, even larger oil discovery was made in nearby Glenn Pool that would lead to Tulsa's golden age of the 1920s and its title as the "Oil Capital of the World". Many early oil companies chose Tulsa for their home base. By 1920, Tulsa was called home to almost one hundred thousand people and four hundred different oil companies. The town boasted daily newspapers, telegraph companies, more than ten thousand telephones, as well as numerous other businesses.

Tulsa had the unenviable title of having hosted the most devastating race riots in U.S. history when, on May 30 1921, a black shoe-shine boy named Dick Rowland, was accused of assaulting Sarah Page. She claimed that Rowland grabbed her arm, causing her to flee in panic and a clerk at a nearby store insisted that Rowland had tried to rape Page. Accounts of the incident circulated among the city's white community during the day and became more exaggerated with each telling.

Rowland was arrested by Tulsa police the following day and the Tulsa Tribune printed a story saying that Rowland had attacked the girl, scratching her hands and face and tearing her clothes. The editorial in the same newspaper that day stated that a hanging was planned for that night. Tightly in the grip of the Ku Klux Klan, Tulsa formed a lynch mob that evening around the courthouse. A group of blacks converged around the courthouse in an attempt to defend Rowland. A white man in the crowd apparently confronted an armed black man and attempted to disarm him. In the ensuing scuffle, the white man was killed and a riot began.

The blacks, outnumbered, began retreating to the business district while truckloads of whites set fires and shot them on sight. Far into the early morning hours of the next day Black Tulsa was looted and burned by white rioters. The Greenwood district, known nationally as "Black Wall Street" for its economic success was a particular target. National Guard troops arrived in Tulsa when the governor declared martial law, and began to round up more than 6,000 black people, placing them in various internment centres such as the baseball stadium, the Convention Hall and the Fairgrounds. Though the violence ended in less than twenty-four, many of the interred were kept for up to eight days. In the wake of the violence, thirty-five city blocks lay in charred ruins, over eight hundred people were treated for injuries, and almost fourteen hundred homes were destroyed. Estimates of the dead range up to three hundred and dozens of black families left the area for more peaceful cities.

Tulsa's oil industries were converted to defence purposes on the outbreak of World War II and it brought another period of growth for the area. Many aviation industries converted their factories to accommodate the war effort, and defence workers poured into the city. An increase in offshore drilling operations, after the war, affected the petroleum industry in Tulsa, but by then, diversification into the aircraft and aerospace industry ensured the city's survival. Today, there are more than three hundred aviation-related companies in the city.

I felt stronger after the break and was better equipped, physically and emotionally, to deal with the city traffic. Even the road surface seemed to have improved and I managed to get some of my spirit back. Crossing the Arkansas River was a big thing, as all river crossings in the US tend to be for a bicycle. Sometimes, the only way across is to take a chance with the traffic and, inevitably, the bridge is narrower than the road leading to or away from it. This means that whatever shoulder exists, shrinks to non-existence and the trip becomes hairy. On this occasion, I was comfortable, off the main highway and I could relax crossing the river on Southwest Blvd. I was resolved to get off the bike as soon as possible, but I wanted to get clear of town first. I spotted a Route 66 railroad attraction three miles beyond the river crossing and scouted it out as a possible camping spot.

I wasn't comfortable being so close to the road and went looking for an alternative. The Daniel Webster High School, across the road, had a communal area with benches and the school was all closed up for the evening – maybe for the holidays – so I picked a bench and sat, quietly, until darkness fell. There was little enough movement and I spread out the sleeping bag on my mat to bring the day to an end.

It's the perennial problem with solo touring – nobody to share the experience with. The evenings and night – between finishing cycling for the day and starting again – can drag. For that reason, I try to keep that time span as short as possible. But it's a trade-off, because there are only a certain number of hours and miles I can cycle before the body breaks down. Other factors limit mileage – road surface, traffic, stress, weather and heat. Then there's the factor of stealth-camping in a built-up area. Hanging around a school would have its risks at the best of times. More and more in the US, I'd been told, homeless men are on bicycles, using them to get out of the centres of population in the evening to find quiet locations for the night. I was a tourist who, despite the, now, scruffy appearance, could afford a hotel room. My present situation was one of choice.

There was some kind of sports practice in the football stadium across the stream from me and the participants and spectators emptied out about nine-thirty. My bike was parked, so as not to appear deliberately hidden, but not so visible as to draw attention either. I began to question the advisability of passing on the Route 66 Village across the street, which, though its singular attraction was an old train of the Tulsa Sapulpa Union Railway, might have been a less suspicious location. Paradoxically, I might have been more visible, but less likely to be disturbed. I was ready for bed, but the few stragglers at the football field delayed my retirement. Finally the last car left and I was left to the darkness. I was tired and my entrance to Tulsa had been the first time on this trip when I'd questioned my sanity. Still, long ago, I'd learnt to believe that events are generally unconnected and that each day should be treated as a separate entity – so I'd sleep on it in the hope and expectation that tomorrow would be better.

Day 11 Fri 10 Jun
Tulsa OK to Davenport OK
Distance 104 km / 65 miles
Total so Far 1456 km / 910 miles
Accommodation: $12.00 Oak Creek RV Park, Davenport OK

Before dawn, I was on the bike, moseying across to the football stadium, just to refill my water bottles. I needed a drink! I'd decided that the unconsumed portion of the previous evening's pizza would serve as a cold breakfast. It was disgusting and did nothing for my humour. Finding the football field open at that hour was a bonus, but there was no water – only a courting couple trying to score on the halfway line before dawn. I left them to their early-morning calisthenics and pedalled onto the route, believing that it might be a dry morning.

To my relief, a gas station presented itself almost immediately and delivered three litres of water – and a bad coffee with a great bagel. Another stressor put aside, I steeled myself for a day of increasing elevation in temperatures that might test. It was barely light when I passed through Sapulpa, a sizeable town of twenty thousand. There was little sign of life in the town known as "The Crossroads of America," sitting at the intersection of U.S. Highway 66 and U.S. Highway 75. Before interstate highways were constructed, Route 66 was the main east-west highway of the western United States and U.S. 75 was the main north-south highway, running from Canada to the Gulf Coast at Galveston, Texas.

I was reluctant to stop in Kellyville, near the bottom of a gentle, freewheeling, descent. The hills in the middle distance indicated that I would be climbing before I got to Bristow, so I decided to get stuck in. The road was quiet, with most of the traffic speeding along the nearby I-44. The only traffic I would have on this stretch was likely to be local traffic so cycling was comfortable. I could take in the sights and smells of the Midwest. The road surface was good and I felt strong enough.

Just short of Bristow, I met Tom on a recumbent. I was on the downhill and I pulled across to say hello. He looked under pressure and said it was his first day on the road, having left from Davenport. His wife had said that he needed to stop thinking about Route 66 – and get on with it. His bike wasn't really suited to the uphills, but would have advantages on the flat or downhill. He was reluctant to get back on the road and I was happy to pass the time. He'd been a leisure cyclist for a number of years and had done a number of multi-day tours. This one – to St Louis – was going to be his longest and was hoping to average about fifty miles a day for the ten or eleven days he had available. He had a brother in Joplin and another in St Louis, so he wasn't going to suffer unduly. He'd driven the route a number of times, but this was going to give him a new perspective. He knew he hadn't put in the training and he was going to suffer until he got fit.

I said goodbye and we parted. I knew, from experience, that the whole trip was likely to be painful. A long tour usually hurts for ten days, until the rhythm becomes established, after which it becomes bearable. I was on my eleventh day now and had begun the tour with a level of fitness that meant my suffering was always likely to be less than on my previous trip. I almost felt a little smug at Tom's initial difficulty. We were all there!

Bristow had a McDonalds, where I plugged in a battery pack and made a Skype call home. One of the primary rules of touring is to establish whether a place has power outlets, toilet paper and WiFi – before ordering coffee. Senior's coffee was still available and I had a spot near the window where I could appreciate the air-conditioning, while watching the bike. I'd over thirty miles done – about half the day's journey – so I could afford to lighten up and enjoy not being melted. The tiredness and grumpiness I'd felt leaving my perch in the morning had dissipated and my mood had lightened considerably. I was invited to join a group of older men, when they saw me sitting alone. They were all ex-military who'd served in Korea or Vietnam and who met up each morning for coffee and war stories. I was reluctant to engage with political chatter, but when they asked me for my feelings about the trip so far, I said that I had really been looking forward to undertaking it during a US Presidential Election year. I'd been disappointed at the lack of political activity along the route, saying that I'd seen more activity in Kentucky in 2014 than I'd seen along the route. It seemed that this election was being fought out on television rather than in reality.

They were all united in their Republicanism and that made their choice difficult. They said that it was almost as if the system had conspired to deliver a candidate that they'd never knowingly vote for, but the alternative – voting Democrat – was unthinkable. They saw Hillary Clinton as the obvious choice and they couldn't imagine that communist, Bernie Sanders, having a chance. These men saw no difficulties with their lives. The Midwest was a place where values were all-important, a place looked down on by city dwellers. Any recovery during the previous eight years was only felt in the major cities, New York, Washington, Chicago, LA and San Francisco. I said that the same seemed to apply in Ireland where any recovery seemed to be in the urban areas. In fact, I said, our Taoiseach, the Prime Minister, had called the people in my locality – where he came from himself – in the West of Ireland, "Whingers" for saying there was no evident recovery.

This was when I first heard of the Electoral College. I'd known that George W. Bush had lost the popular vote to Al Gore, but had won the Presidency. They tried to explain it as best they understood it, but I'm not sure that they understood it themselves. They said that Congressmen and Senator had votes and that the votes of a state were to see how these votes would be cast. I thought that this didn't seem fair – that the candidate getting the most votes might not be the winner. The beauty of the system, they said, was that it meant small states wouldn't always be dictated to by the liberal left, who were more likely to live in the big centres. It was important, they said, to protect their way of life and prevent outside influences from destroying their society. They were passionate about this and all belonged to the "Kids, these days…" age group. They felt the world they knew was changing, that they were losing control, that kids were coming back from college with crazy ideas and not staying. The attractions of the big cities were taking the next generation but, at least, with the Electoral College, those who remained, could fight back.

I wasn't a whole lot wiser, except that I had been aware from the time I left Chicago, that this part of the United States, was pretty much mono-cultural. I'd been in touch with a friend in Boston and had said how impressed I was with the friendliness and generosity of those I'd met. He'd replied that it shouldn't have come as a surprise – that I was nice, on a bicycle and white!

Where Bristow is now, was part of the Creek Indian Nation until, in 1896, the Indians were assigned allotments of land and forced to give up the rest so that the region could be settled by homesteaders. The following year, the St. Louis and San Francisco Railroad began to extend its tracks from Sapulpa to Oklahoma City. A small trading post was established and a post office followed in 1898, named for Kansas Senator Joseph L. Bristow. The railroad arrived in July, 1898, and a small settlement began to grow. The area settlers soon organized and built a small school. In the beginning, most of the area was occupied by Creek Indian owners and white tenant farmers and quickly became known as a little cotton kingdom. Other farms in the surrounding area produced corn, peanuts, potatoes and fruit. In the 1900 census, the population of Bristow was listed as 626. The town continued to grow and over the next decade a number of buildings and businesses were established.

When Oklahoma became a state in 1907, the city was designated as the Creek County Seat, when its population was 1,134. The county held a special election on August 20, 1908 to decide whether the seat would remain in Bristow or move to Sapulpa, which claimed to be more centrally located. Though Bristow had a larger population and claimed to have better railroad connections, Sapulpa won the election. However, Bristow claimed voting irregularities and several years later, the election was voided and a new vote was held November 20, 1912. Once again, Sapulpa won the election which finalised the decision for good.

These were exciting years for Bristow. The town was thriving and Route 66 also rolled through in 1926. This brought many travellers through and the city responded with all types of service businesses. It was also during the 1920's that Gene Autry worked briefly as a telegrapher at the Frisco Depot. He later transferred to Sapulpa and then to the station in Chelsea, where he was discovered by Will Rogers. While awaiting the next train, Rogers noticed Autry's guitar and asked him to play a tune to pass the time. Rogers was so impressed that he mentioned Autry on his national radio show and from then, Autry became one of the biggest country-western stars of the time.

Saying goodbye to these veterans and heading on, I was relaxed. It was still only mid-morning and I'd covered almost half my distance. I could afford to relax, to ensure I wasn't off the road too early. At the same time, I didn't want to be battling the heat. I stopped to have a Coke in Depew, seven miles further on, where I treated my hand with the painful salt in a diner. I couldn't see any significant improvement, but I'd put up with the pain for another few days. A girl waiting for her takeaway chatted to me. She taught yoga in Bristow and I said that, at that moment, I wished I'd learnt yoga – it might stretch out the kinks in my back and legs. She collected her order and left, only to return moments later with a gift for me of a stone ornament of a bullfrog. Just to remember the area, she said. I thanked her and assured her that it would travel with me all the way – and then to Ireland. I never even got her name.

Today, this picturesque small town of just about 550 people is, unfortunately, lined with empty business buildings testifying to more prosperous days. The vast majority of people are employed in jobs in Bristow and Sapulpa. The town still boasts its original 1920's Route 66 concrete pavement running right through the centre of town. There are also several historic buildings to be seen including the old Coppedge Drug Store and the Gimmel Gas Station. Though small, Depew's residents are proud of their history and heritage along the Mother Road.

The frog analogy was apt because today was a series of short hops. From Depew to Stroud was less than twelve miles. A feature of this trip was how close together settlements were. I didn't have the hours of nothingness I'd had in Nevada or Utah – But I could see these looming in the later part of the ride.

Founded in 1892 and named for trader James Stroud, the small town began by selling whiskey to the many cowboys and travellers escaping nearby "dry" Indian Territory. Thirsty for a drink, the town soon boasted nine saloons and became a wild "hell-raising" town, as cattlemen relaxed after days on the range with their herds. Stroud's wild party days soon came to an end when Oklahoma Statehood forced the town "dry" in 1907.

Stroud settled down to a sleepy little town that made its living primarily from agriculture and oil. However, when Route 66 came through town,

Stroud responded like hundreds of other small towns, with services popping up which provided all manner of amenities to the many travellers of the Mother Road.

One such business that still thrives today is the Rock Café, a Route 66 icon. The café, an inspiration of a man named Roy Rieves, began in 1936. Roy had saved his money for most of his life and spent his retirement by starting the popular restaurant when he bought several business lots skirting the city limits of Stroud.

The paving of Route 66 was finishing and business was booming along the highway. Roy built the café almost single-handedly over the next three years, using the very rocks removed from the old road while paving Route 66. Now listed on the National Register of Historic Places, the Rock Cafe is still serving home cooking to Route 66 travellers today. Dawn Welch, owner of the Rock Cafe served as the inspiration to the Sally Carrera character in the 2006 Disney-Pixar animated movie "Cars." A crew from Pixar, researching Route 66 for the film in 2001, stopped for dinner at the Rock Cafe and met Welch.

This was my main-meal stop for the day. I pulled into the town park and occupied the bandstand, lying back in the shade to relax before my lunch. Power outlets, conveniently supplied by the town council charged all my stuff and I napped for forty-five minutes. Only fifteen miles from the day's end at Davenport, I tucked into the plate of steakburger with brown gravy and onions, served with mashed potatoes and green beans. The waitress delivered a pitcher of iced water – and then, another. The place was rocking. I was most surprised to see that no customer was having a beer. Perhaps it was because it was lunchtime, rather than the end of the day. The staff seemed familiar with the clientele, so perhaps it was a normal lunch spot for the locals. It would have warranted a return visit from me – if I was a local.

The 1999 Oklahoma tornado outbreak, which destroyed the town's 53-store Tanger Outlet Center as well as a distribution centre owned by foodservice company Sygma devastated Stroud. Neither of these facilities was rebuilt and the resulting loss of 800 jobs caused significant economic distress to the town.

Stroud's population peaked at 3,148 in 1980, and though the population has fallen since to about 2,700 people today, it is currently enjoying increased economic activity in the oil and gas sectors. Renewed interest in Route 66, and Stroud's strategic location midway between Oklahoma City and Tulsa, contribute to the town's success.

I was sluggish after lunch and was glad to take the time to appreciate Davenport, just about seven miles down the road. The temperatures weren't oppressive and I felt comfortable enough just to cruise around town and take in the sights of this small town of about one thousand souls. I was coming to understand that, while I had set out along Route 66 from Chicago – and my knowledge of the route was confined to iconic pictures of motor transport along the route – Steinbeck had created a monster through his writing. To the casual traveller, it could appear that all the communities along the route came into being because of the building of the route, when, in fact, they all pre-dated the route and it was the creation of I-44 that made them backwaters. It is easy to forget that being on a bicycle gives an extremely skewed appreciation of distances and a place like Davenport – only about fifty miles from Oklahoma City – was no longer distant from anywhere.

Davenport originally had a one-mile stretch of streets paved with brick from a local plant and, even today, six blocks of these old streets are still utilised, and are on the National Register of Historic Places. At about the same time, Davenport's town leaders began to campaign for the routing of a branch of the Ozark Trail Highway through the city. Successful in their efforts, the Ozark Trail was designated in 1916. During the next decade,

Davenport, Stroud, and Chandler merchants would benefit from the publicity surrounding the continuing development of the Ozark Trail. In 1924, the trail became State Highway 7 and just two years later, the highway became Route 66 in 1926.

Two large murals on historic downtown buildings depicting nine scenes were reproduced by professional artists from actual photos from the early days. The 1891 Land Run scene from Harper's Weekly is the tallest mural on Route 66, soaring 32 feet high on the south side of the 1905 Farmers Bank Building. Other scenes are of Nettie Davenport, first postmaster and namesake of the town, her log cabin post office, oil boom scenes, cotton fields and business views.

The last three and a-half miles to Oak Glen RV Park was uphill into a light wind that did nothing to improve my speed. I was happy to get off the bike and get the tent pitched. At sixty-five miles, it was my shortest day to date, but I wasn't complaining as I sat at a picnic table, sipping a Bud Light while taking in my surroundings.

This was the second rural RV Park – that was privately-owned – in the last couple of days. The other had been in Vinita, and neither gave the impression of families on vacation. It seemed far more likely that they were families of seasonal workers, judging from the appearance of the RVs. They looked far more like vehicles in everyday use, rather than machines taken out of storage for a couple of weeks. The kids seemed to have total familiarity with the place – rather than displaying the excitement of discovery and boisterous play. About five in the afternoon, the place came a little more awake, as returning trucks brought life to the place. The occupants, normally wearing work-clothes appeared tired and worn. Nobody exchanged pleasantries with me. I supposed that, being a vacationer, I wasn't in their lives anyway.

With Keith in Chandler

A Facebook message from Keith, an online friend from Perkins OK, had invited me to take a bit of a detour from Route 66 and to take a break with him. It was only thirty miles off-route, but I was thinking that if I was to take time off route – and, by now, I was a couple of days up on my schedule – I would save those days for a possible revisit to Utah later on. I regretfully declined Keith's offer in a Facebook message and, while I was updating my own page, he sent me a reply saying that, if I wasn't too tired, he'd like to drive down to the RV Park and take me to dinner. I accepted his offer and looked forward to like-minded company for a couple of hours. He drove the thirty miles south to my location and brought me to Chandler. I had been urged to go on this town rather than stop at the RV Park, but, with no sign of camping availability, I'd stopped short. The Italian restaurant didn't have a beer licence so we made do with sodas and iced water as we ate our pizzas. A dry town is no place for a thirsty cyclist to stop, so the RV Park had been a good move.

Keith told me of his touring trips, his Transcontinental trip in 2011 and his European adventure with his sons in 2015. We discussed the pros and cons of company. My preference has always been to have a companion – though I've never been so blessed – but I'm acutely aware of the compromises necessary to make this a success. We agreed that solo travelling requires no compromises. Back at the campsite, Keith produced a couple of beers from the coolbox he'd brought with him and we sat a while longer chatting about cycling and his plans for a "bike fort" in Perkins. It seems like a fantastic idea that can only benefit the community.

As usual, despite the enjoyment I was experiencing at having company, by nine o'clock, I was flagging and it was dark and bedtime. Keith said goodnight and I thanked him for a wonderful evening before he left me to my devices – ablutions and checking the area around my tent to ensure all loose ends were tidied. We'd passed a Walmart on the way to Chandler so I knew that I'd be able to get breakfast and supplies in the morning on the way through. I switched out the light on another good day.

Day 12 Sat 11 Jun
Davenport OK to El Reno OK
Distance 138 kms / 86 miles
Total so Far 1594 kms / 996 miles
Accommodation: $50.00 Budget Motel, El Reno OK

Before Keith had left, we'd discussed my options for the following day. One thing was certain, I was not going to stay in Oklahoma City so the decision was whether to stop short in Edmond or push through to El Reno. Either way, I would be going uphill, gradually, for the day.

Chandler has, no doubt, a number of attractions. I'd failed to see or feel its Route 66 vibe the evening before and this morning, I was focused on worshipping at the altar of Walmart. I had a few dehydrated meals, but one of the rules of touring is to buy these meals and figure out how to avoid eating them! I got a sandwich and coffee in McDonalds and a few bits in Walmart and continued through the lifeless town. But, then again, it was only six in the morning.

From its beginning until the mid-1920's, the production of cotton and related activities were the most important sources of income for the citizens of Chandler. From age six, children learned to pick cotton, and many continued this throughout their lives. Full attendance at school for older children could not be expected before mid-November, after the entire cotton crop was harvested.

Bill Tilghman, one of the pioneers making the land rush in 1891 and former marshal of Dodge City, was elected sheriff of Lincoln County in 1900. He would later serve as United States Marshal and became known as "Two-Gun Bill" and he was largely responsible for wiping out organized crime in Oklahoma and hunting down Bill Doolin and his gang. Though the area was quickly advancing into the twentieth century, it was seemingly not quite finished with its Old West heritage and Tilghman, though retired had been prevailed on to become city marshal of Cromwell, Oklahoma, an Oil Boomtown about 50 miles southeast of Chandler. On November 1, 1924 Tilghman was eating in a restaurant when a shot was fired outside by a drunken Prohibition Officer, by the name of Wiley Lynn. At the sound of the shot, Tilghman immediately left the restaurant and began to lead Lynn toward the jail. Lynn, who had clashed with Tilghman on other occasions, pulled out a small automatic pistol and shot Tilghman, who died 15 minutes later. The incident is recognized as one of the last gunfights of the Old West. Tilghman is buried at the Oak Park Cemetery just west of Chandler.

When the Mother Road came through Chandler in 1926 it brought a significant amount of commercial business as travellers crossed the state and the country. When the turnpikes began to be built, Chandler like many Route 66 cities suffered another blow. However, agriculture and livestock have continued to keep this small community of almost three thousand alive today.

I'd underestimated my need for company and the good feeling that remained from Keith's visit sustained me to Arcadia, thirty miles away. On the way, I passed through the ghost town of Warwick and, beyond there, the small communities of Wellston and Luther, before arriving at the Round Barn in Arcadia, built in 1898, the most photographed building on all of Route 66. The brainchild of William Harrison Odor, locals scoffed at the idea of a round barn, but Odor soaked green lumber in water and shaped the rafters to form the exact curve of the roof. When his masterpiece was complete, he utilized the lower level to store his hay and shelter cattle and mules, while the upper level was used for barn dances and social gatherings.

By the 1980's the barn had begun to suffer from years of neglect and was donated to the Arcadia Historical and Preservation Society in an effort to save it. Luther Robinson, a retired building contractor from Oklahoma City, restored the barn with the help of a volunteer group known as the "Over-the-Hill-Gang."

The Round Barn

The now-closed HillBillee's BBQ at the entrance to the small town was once the home of an original Route 66 Gas Station, Café and Motor Court. Legend has it that in the early years of Route 66, the motor court would even provide a "companion" for male travellers. They don't appear to have catered for cyclists.

Pops convenience store and restaurant, on the city's west edge, is a popular new addition to Arcadia's tourism landscape. It was built by fracking mogul Aubrey McClendon and designed by renowned Oklahoma architect Rand Elliott. It's now a major modern roadside attraction on Route 66. Opened in 2007, using a theme of soda pop, it is marked by a giant neon sign in the shape of a soda pop bottle. The glass walls of the restaurant are decorated with shelves of soda pop bottles, arranged by colour. Apparently, there are five hundred flavours. The roadside sign is 66 feet tall – a reference to the historic highway. Although apparently constructed from neon tubes, it is actually lit by LEDs, providing a spectacular light show each night. Of more immediate concern to me was the fact that it served food in a nice clean environment – and it had free WiFi in its diner-style restaurant. I'd been told that it was a "must" along the route. From a scale point of view, it didn't disappoint, but it was packed with visitors and the food was a bit pricey.

The mind behind the enterprise, fifty-eight year-old McClendon, died in a single-vehicle crash in Oklahoma City on 02 March 2016, the day after he'd been indicted by a federal grand jury on charges of conspiring "to rig bids for the purchase of oil and natural gas leases in northwest Oklahoma".

The temperatures had been rising in the last couple of days and it was in the high eighties Fahrenheit as I pulled away from Pops after my early lunch. I was now firmly in tornado country and was aware how these high temperatures could trigger different weather patterns. It was normal for this time of year, but I'd known that when setting out. I was always going to hit varying weather conditions over the length of the route. The fact that I was conserving my water might have led to me being hot and bothered when I reached Edmond. I searched for somewhere to take a break, but there seemed a complete absence of public parks. I found a single picnic table on, what in winter might have been a green area, but was now a brown spot. Resting my head on my arms, I got thirty minutes of a rest, before facing into the traffic again.

I think it was the relentless noise of crazy exhausts, combined with weekend traffic and the added heat generated by the asphalt and cement that had me on edge. The complete absence of anyone from whom to get directions only served to compound my isolation – only fools were not availing of air-conditioning today. Finally I took a wrong turn and ended up on a small street behind a car that I thought was in traffic. As I waited for it to move, I looked around at the small, neat properties. The car seemed to take a long time in moving off and it was only then that I noticed that it was actually parked. I needed to get out of the sun! A couple at the door of one of the houses filled a water bottle for me and I got going again.

In Downtown Oklahoma City, stands a reminder to the four thousand-pound truck-bomb on April 19, 1995, that destroyed one-third of the Alfred P. Murrah Federal Building, killed one hundred and sixty-eight people and injured almost seven hundred. The blast destroyed or damaged hundreds of buildings within a sixteen-block radius and destroyed or burned cars, causing an estimated $652 million worth of damage. The bombing was carried out by Timothy McVeigh and Terry Nichols. McVeigh was executed by lethal injection in 1991, while his co-accused, Nichols received one hundred and sixty-one life sentences without parole. The Oklahoma City Outdoor Symbolic Memorial stands where the federal building used to stand and is as evocative as any war cemetery in Europe. It demands reflection. One of its constituent parts is the "Survivor Tree". The American Elm Tree, more than ninety years old, survived the bomb's blast. Before the bombing, the tree had been important because it provided the only shade in the downtown parking lot. People would arrive early to work just to be able to park under the shade of the tree's branches. On the day I visited, I could appreciate their actions. In the aftermath of the bombing, the tree was almost chopped down to recover pieces of evidence that hung from the branches and the trunk of the tree due to the force of bomb.

When hundreds of community citizens, family members of those who were killed, survivors and rescue workers came together to write the Memorial Mission Statement, one of its resolutions dictated that "one of the components of the Memorial must be the Survivor Tree located on the south half of the Journal Record Building block."

Mark Bays, an urban forester with the Oklahoma Department of Agriculture, Food and Forestry, developed a plan to save the tree and took it on as a project for years. The asphalt that lined the parking lot was pulled away from the tree to begin improving the conditions around it. Seeds were taken and seedlings were grown. The tree began to thrive.

This old elm became a prominent feature of The Memorial design, unveiled in 1996, and, because the roots of the tree ran so deep, the promontory was put on piers to avoid damage to the tree's root system. Each pier was hand dug by Bays and the construction crew. The design also included an aeration and irrigation system underneath the promontory, which permits the air and water to get underneath the tree's roots. This state of the art system allows the tree to receive the appropriate amount of water and air to keep it growing for years to come. I don't think any tree – since the apple tree in the Garden of Eden – has received so much attention!

Cuttings of the Survivor Tree are growing in nurseries all over Oklahoma. Owners of landscape nurseries, urban foresters and expert horticulturists from across the state and country have come together to work and preserve this piece of history. None of these people have ever charged the Memorial for their work. Each year, seeds are harvested and planted, generating saplings to be distributed on the anniversary of the bombing. Today, thousands of Survivor Trees are growing in public and private places all over the United States.

The afternoon was getting on and I was still almost thirty miles from El Reno. I could have found a motel somewhere in town, but I have an aversion to big centres of population while I'm on the bike. In addition, there's a greater likelihood of bike theft in urban centres, so I carried on in what I figured was the approximate direction.

Two girls out for a cycle directed me onto a trail and it was great to get out of the traffic for about fourteen miles before coming out on Yukon Parkway and recovering Route 66. I drank a lot of Coke in the 7 Eleven attached to the gas station before turning back onto East Main Street. I was mightily relieved that I had only about another two hours of cycling left. The Route 66 landscape of rundown motels and fast food outlets reasserted itself and, as I cycled along the street, I was hailed from what looked like a small park on my right. I needed a rest anyway and I pulled in. It was a ramshackle gazebo in front of a rundown motel that typically let rooms by the week.

Two people were sitting there in the shade and I was invited to take a seat and share a beer – all of which I did. Five o'clock was time enough to be off the bike and I was sorely tempted by Dawn's offer of a patch of grass where I could pitch the tent. She was the manageress of this motel and a former truck driver. Her voice carried the echo of every cigarette she'd ever smoked and her face reflected her time on the road in a male-dominated industry. She'd been working at a rest stop on an interstate originally, but the boredom got to her. She'd envied the drivers passing through, with their stories of the open road, the independence and the freedom from the agenda of others. She applied and was accepted. She said that, despite the low numbers of female truck drivers, it was an equal-opportunity employer and her safety record enabled her to advance.

She'd been driving for over forty years. She started with her husband back in the sixties, but he died in an accident in 1978. Since then, Dawn had been driving mostly solo. She has had a few team partners but has always preferred driving alone. There was a lot of change over the years. "Most men back then would rather have had a hot coal dropped in their pocket than to offer assistance." She said that if you "act like a lady you will be treated like a lady" and once accepted by the men on equal terms, the men became fiercely protective. She set herself apart from the men with one of her favourite trucks; it was "black and hot pink with pink butterflies on both sides." By decorating her truck with colours and symbols that are considered feminine, Dawn made it clear that there was a woman behind the wheel, challenging the viewpoint of truck drivers as masculine. The other benefit was that the men wouldn't be seen dead driving her truck – so it stayed clean. Dawn laughs and takes another swig of beer, before becoming serious and telling me of the hardships of being on the road. Once the romance of the "freedom of the open road" wears off, men and women face different as well as the same hardships in their lives as truck drivers. They have to leave behind children, spouses and families in order to do their job. Driving a truck is a truck is a team and family effort, and if either team or family doesn't buy into it, the future is bleak. Dawn lost out in the crash of 2008 and went to live with her daughter initially. She had become so accustomed to being on her own that it didn't work out. She got depressed, started drinking and finally had to leave.

She'd gotten herself together in the last few years and, now, was running this place. Was she happy? "Dunno, I've been here five years and I don't want to move no more. I have my memories and if'n I close my eyes, I can still feel the cab moving on the open road and I can smell the air. I sure as hell don't miss the crap food at gas stations or the nights spent on the road, broken down!" She asked me about my trip and I said that our experiences might not be that different – except that I was doing it as a vacation, not as a way of living. That took a lot of pressure off, but I'd spent time on the road, not knowing where I'd stop, what I'd eat, or who I'd run into. As long as I did it because I wanted to, I'd enjoy it. Once it became something I'd be obliged to do, I'd stop.

I was sorely tempted to stop for the evening. There was a wind getting up and it might bring a storm, but here, I would be still in an urban setting and I'd feel I still hadn't escaped Oklahoma City. Anyway, the wind had all the hallmarks of a tailwind – and I'd never miss out on that. I thanked

Dawn for the beer, patted the mongrel dog who'd been nosing around my bags, and left to head on down the road – another fourteen, mostly uphill miles, to El Reno.

The wind got stronger and pushed me on. I felt good after the break and the chat, feeling that, through Dawn, I'd made a connection with Route 66 that had been missing. By the time I got to El Reno, the wind had strengthened from my left, bringing stinging particles of sand and making the bike difficult to control. I worried a little about the peals of thunder and the flashes of lightning to the south. Whatever was down there, was heading in my direction and I wasn't sure how quickly. I was certain of one thing, though – this weather was going to be a new departure for me and I wasn't going to be in a tent when it hit. I took the motel option for safety – if for no other reason than to get the dust and sweat out of my clothes.

El Reno was built at the intersection of two historic highways – the Old Chisholm Trail and Route 66. Before the town of El Reno was born, a man by the name of Jesse Chisholm established the Chisholm Trail in 1866, where hundreds of herds of cattle would be driven north from Texas to Kansas where they would be loaded on trains headed east.

In the same year the Cheyenne-Arapaho Reservation was established by a treaty negotiated, in part by Black Kettle, considered the greatest chief of the Southern Cheyenne but later killed by General George Custer at the Battle of the Washita near the present town of Cheyenne. The Cheyenne and Arapaho tribes were moved from eastern Colorado to land south of the Arkansas River. Fort Reno was established in 1874, to quell the unrest among the Indians in the region and was named Fort Reno in 1876 in honour of Major General Jesse L. Reno, who had been killed in the Civil War. The soldiers soon built a stockade where Lieutenant General Philip Sheridan conducted his Indian campaigns from headquarters established at the fort. The United States Cavalry units calmed down the uprisings in the area, but, stayed on to maintain the peace.

When Route 66 was built, El Reno, like hundreds of its counterpart cities, quickly obliged its many travellers with a crop of restaurants, motels and service stations along the road. Route 66 followed Rock Island Avenue and turned onto Choctaw Avenue before directing me on Sunset Drive. The Budget Inn of El Reno is, according to its blurb, "close to the Lucky Star Casino, El Reno Federal Prison and Fort Reno and much more. The hotel features 24-hour front desk wireless Internet access guest laundry and parking." Well, the bike would join me in the room and what really sold it for me was the Sonic fast food outlet almost across the street and the liquor store beside it. I would definitely use the Sonic – and maybe stop off to buy a beer.

I was nearly one thousand miles into my journey and, so far, the weather had been kind. The road conditions had been good and generally not too difficult. I hadn't had to deal with the wind that others had warned me of, advising me to travel from west to east. If today's late afternoon wind was a foretaste of things to come, I could see myself waiting out the weather for a day or two and I'd be glad of the days I'd built up.

I showered, did my laundry and headed off for food. There's so little difference between all the fast food establishments that one would have to wonder at their survival. The burger didn't lend itself to a lot of contemplation – at that stage it was only about eating. The Liquor Store was closed as I made my way back to my room and I was glad that, as a source of temptation, it was gone. They don't break sixpacks and I didn't want to be carrying the unconsumed portion. I was half tempted to head the half-a-mile back to the centre of town to Gilmore's Pub & Barefoot Bar, but, though it might be my first time to visit an authentic bar since Divernon, IL, I skipped it and settled for channel surfing on the old television. This motel didn't pay a subscription for cable, obviously, as the choice of content was abysmal. I finally settled on a news channel which was giving a bit of information of the US Presidential Election. Hillary

Clinton was having a greater battle than expected with Bernie Sanders, while Donald Trump, formerly a seemingly joke candidate, had seen off the opposition, John Kasich, Ted Cruz, Marco Rubio, Jeb Bush and the others. With no obvious posters along the route, if I hadn't turned on the TV, I'd never have known there was an election. I hadn't discussed politics much along the way – but nobody indicated an intention to vote for Hillary Clinton. I turned off the television and slept!

Day 13 Sun 12 Jun
El Reno OK to Clinton, OK
Distance 116 kms / 72.5 miles
Total so Far 1710 kms / 1068.5 miles
Accommodation: Free – ish Campsite in Clinton OK

I broke one thousand miles for my trip so far, today. It was a thing of nothing – just another figure on the odometer – but it indicated progress. I woke at four-thirty – and promptly fell back to sleep. So much for getting on the road before dawn and missing the heat!

Packed up and on the road by, seven, I revisited Sonic for breakfast and, with half of it stowed in my bar bag, headed west on Sunset Drive, past the businesses that were either auto-focused or farming-oriented. I was getting more of a feel for Steinbeck's family, the Joads, going west to California. They'd started out from Sallisaw, near the state line with Arkansas and had been on a parallel route with me – but to the south – until Oklahoma City, when they joined Route 66. Steinbeck was the first to call it "The Mother Road"

Steinbeck's magnum opus is obsessed with what the narrator calls the "citadel of the family" and demonstrates the bonds that unite blood relations despite twists of fate and ill-fortune. I was finding the epic story of the Joad family struggling against all odds to survive, profoundly touching and compelling. John Ford, Bruce Springsteen and Woody

Guthrie were all equally caught up in his work. Its exhortations to socialism are there throughout, but there is also a righteous anger, determined to keep the reader uncomfortable. Even in the early days of this book, I kept hoping that Steinbeck would give the characters a break. With great recession-induced austerity currently hitting the worst-off throughout the western world, this Great Depression-era tale of have-nots being at the whim of faceless corporations and blood-sucking banks has special resonance. In every fragile society, it is the "have-leasts" who suffer disproportionately, whether it's escaping from war-torn Syria, fleeing genocide in Rwanda, or ethnic-cleansing in Kosovo. The author said that he wanted his book to "rip a reader's nerves to rags" and he certainly managed that with me.

I'd been getting into the book over the past few days, having deliberately waited until Oklahoma to start it. My only concession to extra weight, I'd found it to have been an inspired choice, leaving me angry and animated with each turned page.

The sky to the south looked dark and threatening as I cycled with the wind on my back. The original Route 66 had bypassed the small communities of Calumet, Geary and Bridgeport so that they'd had to get surviving or get dead. Bridgeport is pretty much a ghost town today and I passed to the south of the other towns so I can't testify as to their success. Where the route leaves the alignment of the interstate – the I-40 had replaced the I-44 as my companion – before Bridgeport, there is a spur going off to the north. The more I looked at it on the map, the more I realised that I was adding needless miles, so I took the left turn that kept me on the very original Route 66. I should have known better!

The surface left a lot to be desired and I climbed a hill that, legend says, many of the old Model A's and Model T's had to climb in reverse in order to generate enough power to get up. I was enjoying the fast, but rocky, descent when I heard something fall from the bike. Fearing the worst, I stopped and walked back up the incline to where my phone lay in three parts – body, back and battery – along the road. Amazingly, apart from a split screen, it suffered only abrasions and worked fine when reassembled. Breathing a huge sigh of relief, I resolved to make sure that the bar bag remained tightly zipped shut from now on. What would I have done if the phone had been damaged beyond use? Even payphones had disappeared these days, and my means of keeping in touch with home would have been gone. Getting a new phone would have been a hassle until I got to a big town. Even getting one, while not having a permanent address or a bank account, might have posed difficulties. No point in focusing on negatives, I pedalled onwards, a little more cautiously.

I crossed a bridge spanning the Canadian River. Apparently, it has thirty-eight trusses and, built in 1933, forms a nearly four thousand-foot span. It's the longest truss bridge in the state of Oklahoma and was built along the newer section of Route 66 that bypassed Calumet, Geary and Bridgeport. Properly referred to as the Canadian River Bridge, the west end of the span appeared in the "The Grapes of Wrath." This was the scene where Grandpa dies and is buried. I stopped and rested to reflect on this. The trip was becoming real now.

The road wound through the Oklahoma countryside and I enjoyed the quietness of being a little separated from the interstate on my left. At a service stop, where I had a mid-morning snack, I queued up for my food. A television delivered mute pictures of some significant event. I asked the man behind me, but he didn't know. The girl, who took my money said something had happened in Florida. Then she turned to the next customer. I tried to get an understanding, but it would be a few hours before, I would find out that, on the previous night, Omar Mateen, a 29-year-old security guard, killed forty-nine people and wounded more than fifty in a terrorist attack/hate crime inside Pulse, a gay nightclub in Orlando, Florida. He was shot and killed by Orlando Police Department officers after a three-hour standoff. Pulse was hosting Latin Night and most of the victims were Latino. It was both the deadliest mass shooting by a single shooter and the deadliest incident of violence against LGBT people in United States history. It was also the deadliest terrorist attack in the United States since the September 11 attacks in 2001. Mateen swore allegiance to the leader of the Islamic State of Iraq and the Levant (ISIL), Abu Bakr al-Baghdadi, and said the shooting was "triggered" by the U.S. killing of Abu Waheeb in Iraq the previous month.

It brought home to me the extent to which, by being on the road, I was disconnected from daily news. I'd no doubt but that the forthcoming referendum in Britain over whether or not to remain in the European Union, was making the main headlines at home. Here, it wasn't an issue. On the other hand, what had happened in Orlando would be big news in Ireland – but in Hydro OK, it might have been in another world.

No fuel available – nor needed!

Route 66 bypassed Hydro and on the outskirts there stands Lucille's Historic Highway – a Route 66 attraction which attracts a steady stream of tourists. Christened "The Mother of the Mother Road", in July, 1997, Lucille's station was placed on the National Historic Register. Today, this classic old gas station is only one of two upper-story overstyle stations left on Oklahoma's ribbon of the route. Route 66 enthusiast Rick Koch shored up the gas station building in 2007 as a photo-op and built the popular Lucille's Roadhouse restaurant in nearby Weatherford in tribute.

For me, once I got the photograph taken of Surly resting against the disused gas pumps of the beautifully restored Phillips 66 store, the shaded picnic table was an irresistible lure and I plonked myself there. The place was no longer in operation so I was unlikely to affect trade. A car pulled up and the couple that emerged were, clearly, tourists. Derek and Anita were from Northhamptonshire in the UK. They were supporters of Leicester Tigers rugby team, so we had a bit of a chat about the sport. Derek was a regular traveller to Ireland for the internationals and said how much he always Dublin. It was a great stop before lunch, but I had to be getting on.

At Weatherford, Lucille's Roadhouse, provided lunch. I worried that I was settling – a little too easily – into tourist mode. I banished the thought, along with three pints of iced water, the chicken strips and the fries. It was only alright, but I suppose the Michelin starred food isn't likely to be served up at Kate Kearney's Cottage!

Only fifteen miles separated me from my stop for the day, so I wasn't in a great rush. The map showed Hargus RV Park in Clinton and I put the address into the Garmin and headed off. It wasn't as if I was going to get lost – my road was just over the fence from the I-40 and the traffic was incessant. In an effort to save me from myself, Mr. Garmin took me on a rural tour of the roads north of Route 66, adding ten miles of heat to my day. I took a rest on an embankment, where I slept for half an hour, before being woken by a passing motorist, concerned for my wellbeing. Not many bicycle tourists along this country road, she said – "and when I saw you lying there, I thought that maybe the heat had gotten to you." I thanked her for her concern and she headed off. I got back on the bike, with a close watch on my water levels. I made a mental note – the days were approaching when more weight would be added to my gear as I'd have to carry a good deal more water to sustain me along through the rough terrain in my immediate future.

A girl, probably in her twenties, was washing a car in front of a house some miles further on, so I stopped and asked her if she might fill a water bottle for me. She called to a man in the house to ask if was okay. He checked me out and gave permission. With a full bottle and thoughts of a failed feminist movement, I carried on and intersected with a main road beside Custer County Jail, at Arapaho, where the welcome country store provided an ice-cold Pepsi to sustain me for the last seven miles.

In Clinton, the Oklahoma Route 66 Museum in Clinton offers visitors a "personal journey through the history of the nation's most revered highway. Encounter the iconic ideas, images, and myths of the Mother Road. Learn about the dreams and the labour needed to make the road a reality. Experience the Dust Bowl as thousands streamed along the road, away from drought and despair, and towards the "land of promise." Listen to the sounds of the Big Band era, when the roar of the big trucks and the welcome-home cries to returning soldiers dominated the road. Sit at the counter or a booth in the 1950s diner and feel the open road as America's families vacationed along the length of Route 66." It seemed to focus on cars and I felt I was getting the authentic "Dust Bowl" experience from Steinbeck, so I didn't take them up on the offer. On a Sunday afternoon, I would have been worried about leaving the bike unattended, so I wouldn't have managed to get the full experience. Across the street from the museum, the Tradewinds Best Western Inn was once a favourite of Elvis Presley, and further on down the line, the promised Jiggs Smoke House, a small cabin cafe that's been selling barbecue for years, was closed.

A sign for the Holiday Inn Express, indicated the presence of a campsite and I was expecting the same facility and price as I'd experienced in Marshfield MO. It would also be on my way out of town in the morning – and the presence of an Aquapark with slides and pools was an added attraction. I shifted from my original plan to explore – fully intent, before evening registering, that I'd take a day off the bike. The girl on reception said it was $58.95 per night for me and my tent.

"Are you sure?" says I.
"Yes", says she.
"No", says I.

With thoughts of a cool swim evaporating like the perspiration from my body, I climbed on Surly again and pedalled around to Hargus RV Park – an altogether less salubrious field where RVs were parked on small sites. I went to the office – closed. Nobody around, so I just pitched my tent, before heading to the washrooms – only to find a code on the door. Unless someone came along later, I wouldn't be showering. Luckily, the gas station on the road nearby had a restroom and I had a wash before buying some food. Back at the camp, I just relaxed while waiting for camp management to arrive. The price for a tent was $15.00, which was fine – if I had access to the washroom. Nobody arrived, so no money changed hands.

Fifteen miles along the road, the map indicated a KOA campsite. That distance wouldn't constitute a violation of the Rest Day, I'd promised myself, so I'd head off for there in the morning. I was feeling strong, in general, since the trip began, so I had more difficulty in getting my head around the thoughts of a day's inactivity, than I was with the decision to take a day off the bike.

Day 14 Mon 13 Jun
Clinton, OK to Elk City OK / Foss KOA Campsite
Distance 32 kms / 20 miles
Total so Far 1742 kms / 1088.5 miles
Accommodation: $27.00 Campsite in Foss OK

Lots of thunder – and flashes of lightning visible through the walls of my tent kept me awake for a few hours. I finally slept, but at three in the morning, I couldn't sleep any longer. By four I was packed and ready and delayed only to get a bite of breakfast at the gas station. A sausage and egg croissant with coffee and a muffin was as close to a healthy start as I was likely to get at that hour and I looked at the brightening sky – which wasn't! As light came up, I could see the rain clouds. Last night's storm had stayed to the south, but I wasn't sure for how much longer. Still, it was only twenty miles, so I got going.

With an eye to the weather, I passed by the Holiday Inn Waterpark and silently gave it the fingers. I'd had a free night in a campsite, even if I'd had no facilities. There was little or no traffic and I was made good headway on the frontage road. I was pedalling hard, because I knew I'd be getting off the bike. There was no chance of shelter if I got hit by the inevitable storm, so I just kept an eye on the sky as I went – and hoped for the best. About a mile out from the KOA campsite, the rain started but I got to the doorway of the camp management office before the worst of it hit. The temperatures plummeted and I pulled a warm jacket from my pack. The sign on the door told me that the office would be staffed from eight, so I had an hour to wait as the rain came in sideways to where I was trying to stay dry.

Right on time, the staff arrived and I could get out of the elements. The lady took my registration and I hung around a while until the worst seemed to have passed. She even gave me a coffee at no charge, while I stared out the window at the rain. When it had eased off enough to have steam rise from the ground, I set up the tent and got in just in time before the next onslaught of rain kept me prisoner for two hours.

The tent proved equal to the storm on this occasion, but I was concerned that these weather events were of an order to which I was unaccustomed. I might be looking for motels from here on. Finally, it eased off enough for me to consider showering and cleaning up. My towel smelled of alcohol and, on checking my bags, I found that my fuel bottle had split and leaked fuel all over my breakfast foodstuff. I still had my dehydrated meals – but no longer had the means to heat water for them. Luckily, the campsite served food too. Not great, but it would do, in a pinch.

The campsite cleared out quickly. I'd normally left campsites before they emptied, but this was the first time I'd taken up residence at the beginning of the day. Soon I was left almost alone in the place. It was a very long day, spent wandering in and out of the "games" room where a television showed a local news channel. The weather was played out on screen much as I'd seen it and it seemed to be hanging around Clinton. It should move off to the east in the evening. That would suit me fine. I could look forward to a dry day tomorrow.

I lounged and read some of Steinbeck while dozing in an armchair. I went for frequent drinks of water to bring my hydration levels back to where they should be. I'd been neglecting that, because I'd just gotten used to the heat. Not a great idea. I settled for a pizza for dinner and was in bed by nine, just as it was getting dark.

I woke at midnight. A really strong wind was buffeting the tent and I felt that, even if the rain stayed away, it was unlikely to survive the increasing intensity. In a matter of minutes, I had packed the sleeping mat, bag and pillow and got the tent down, with no thoughts to tidiness. I did have to be methodical, though every fibre of my body was telling me to get it done. I didn't want to lose pegs or anything else. I got it to the washroom, where I packed it properly. All my other kit was in waterproof panniers, so I didn't have to worry about it. Whatever about the comfort of my surroundings, I was happy to be out of the rain. I opened the door and watched the light show. The time between flashes and thunder had diminished to almost zero. I wasn't about to go out in the weather to recover the bike – the steel frame wouldn't attract me half as much as it might attract lightning!

A couple had come onto the site about six in the evening and had made a bit of a meal of setting up their tent. I'd been observing them take half an hour to pitch it and, then, they'd stocked it with sleeping bags, lights and pillows from the car. They looked like camping wasn't what they were used to, so I wondered how they were getting on now. My rain jacket was on the front rack and that was the only thing that made me recover the bike during a lull in the storm. A further two trips saw me reunited with my gear and I just sat in the shelter to wait out the rest of the storm. Two hours later, about four in the morning, I saw the couple leave the campsite, their car full of an untidy mess as they hurried away from this encounter with the great outdoors. I wondered if this was the end of a beautiful relationship with camping – if not with each other.

I'd recovered my chair and deployed it in the washroom. It wasn't the most comfortable or luxurious of surroundings, but at least, I was dry. The light was on a timer and would go off every three minutes or thereabouts, so I had to make a movement to be picked up by the sensor. I didn't want to be in the dark if someone came in. Seeing me sitting there as the lights came on might be too much for any half-asleep person answering a call of nature.

At five o'clock, someone came into the washroom and I took this as a cue that it had eased somewhat outside and vacated my shelter. There was a bit of shelter – it might have been a bus shelter – at the front of the building, from where I could observe the light show and the driving rain. It amazed me how fast the traffic was going despite the conditions of very limited visibility. I was certainly not taking my chances on the road – not because it was too wet, but because I wouldn't be seen by drivers. Anyway, there was no rush. By my reckoning, I was, at this stage, about five days ahead of schedule. This wasn't because I'd been doing superhuman day – though I'd done a few that had been longer than initially planned – but because I hadn't been taking the planned rest days. These are built in to cater for tiredness, primarily, but when not required, they're vital as a contingency plan for breakdowns, bad weather or injury.

For those who might imagine bicycle-touring to be an inexact science, you would be quite wrong. There are constant adjustments to be made, to mileages, hours in the saddle, camping locations and so on. But the most important issue is not to arrive at the finish either too early or too late. In 2014, I'd arrived in Boston five days ahead of schedule and had been kicking my heels, waiting for my flight home, while paying more than I'd hoped for accommodation. At the current rate of progress, I could arrive in San Francisco on the 14th of July and not fly out until the 22nd. That wouldn't do. Henry, a friend made in Nevada in 2014 and living in the Bay Area, had offered to host me when I reached the end. I expected to spend three nights with him at the outside. We'd stayed in touch since our shared mileage through Nevada and Utah and I was really looking forward to seeing himself and Danielle again but Five days is more than any host could bear. I had a couple of options that might have to be considered in the next few days.

In Blanding UT, I'd stayed a night with the Lyman family in 2014. Patty and Bruce had been wonderful hosts and I'd maintained contact on Facebook since then. Patty had invited me to come and stay with them again on my trip west, but, at best, it was almost two hundred miles off route. Depending on availability of services – water, food, camping possibilities – that could be three to four days in each direction. She had offered to meet with me in Flagstaff and that would be great. As she had seen my progress on Facebook, she was talking about coming down to collect me and bring me back to spend the Fourth of July with them in Blanding. That might be nice too. I'd keep my options open because the last thing I needed was to feel trapped, or that I was imposing. Never having to say you're sorry is one of the benefits of solo touring!

As I sheltered from the driving rain, the wind died down, only to shift direction. I'd been in the middle of the storm and now it seemed to be passing over. By, six-thirty, I was contemplating my escape. I'd learnt a few rules of touring and the main one for me is that it doesn't matter what speed I do – as long as it's in a forward direction. If I only managed twenty miles today, that would be okay. The red sky of dawn was appearing in the east, the main lightning activity was to the south and I was headed west – away from the misery. Seven o'clock seemed bright enough to be seen on the road and, wrapped up against the chill, like a ship leaving harbour, I climbed on Surly and pulled away from the shelter of the office.

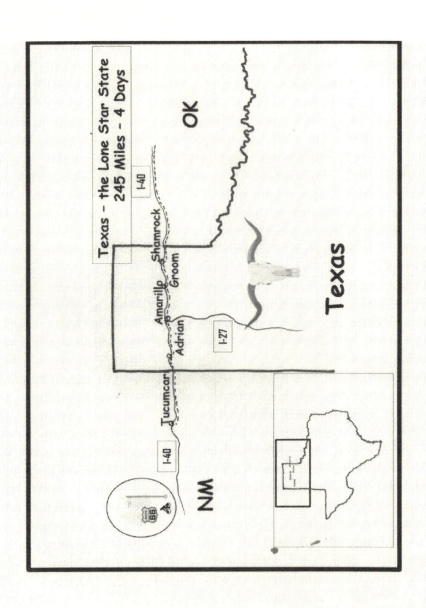

Chapter 5

Texas – The Lone Star State

Day 15 Tue 14 Jun
Elk City / Foss KOA Campsite to Shamrock TX
Distance 118 kms / 74 miles
Total so Far 1860 kms / 1162.5 miles
Accommodation: $3.00 Primitive Campsite

In Elk City, I found a branch of my favourite store – Ace Hardware – and replenished my fuel stock. I'd Googled it and put the address in the Garmin to save time looking for it. Klean Strip de-natured alcohol – what we in Ireland call methylated spirits – is an excellent fuel for the Trangia. It burns cleanly and, more importantly, under control. The mini-Trangia, I'd brought with me was small, light and, to my mind, useless. I wished for my normal one which was sitting in storage at home. At this stage, I wouldn't have minded the extra bulk – the weight difference on the bike was no big deal. The mini had no windshield, so it was hard on fuel when there was even the slightest breeze. Still, while I'd learnt a lesson, I had to make do with what I had. On the way out of town, the Homeland store allowed me to replace my alcohol-sodden foodstuffs – I just hoped the staff in the campsite I'd left didn't use naked flames around the garbage cans for a while!

Elk City, Oklahoma is a town filled with history, from tales of the Old West, to Route 66, to the oil boom days of the early 1980s. My journey west through Oklahoma had been a succession of days when the towns I'd passed through had been the result of displacement of the indigenous people – but that might have been too simplistic. The Native American population on the plains here would not, at that time, have had the technology to exploit the oil reserves. Nor would they have had the interest in herding cattle. In the clash of cultures, they were always going to lose out and, today, I could see from my maps that the area to the west of me would deliver its share of casinos, from which the Indian Nations derive their main income.

Before this part of Indian Territory was opened up to settlement, thousands of head of cattle were driven over the "Great Western Trail" from Texas on their way to Dodge City, Kansas. However, in 1892, the surplus land of the Cherokee Outlet was opened and settlers began to filter into the area. The first pioneer who settled on what would one day become Elk City was named J.M. "Joe" Allee who homesteaded a quarter section of land just east of Elk Creek in 1897. A section equates to one square mile or six hundred and forty acres. A quarter section is 160 acres and a "quarter-quarter section" is 40 acres. In 1832 the smallest area of land that could be acquired was reduced to the 40-acre quarter-quarter section, and this size parcel became entrenched in American mythology. After the Civil War, Freedmen (freed slaves) were reckoned to be self-sufficient with "40 acres and a mule." In the 20th century real estate developers preferred working with 40-acre parcels. The phrases "front 40" and "back 40," referring to farm fields, indicate the front and back quarter-quarter sections of land.

One of the reasons for creating sections of 640 acres was the ease of dividing into halves and quarters while still maintaining a whole number of acres. A section can be halved seven times in this way, down to a 5-acre parcel, or half of a quarter-quarter-quarter section. This system was of great practical value on the American frontier, where surveyors often had a shaky grasp of mathematics and were required to work quickly.

In March of 1901, the Choctaw Townsite and Improvement Company purchased land from Allee, anticipating the arrival of the Choctaw and

Gulf Railroad later that year. Wasting no time, the town site company filed a survey of plotted lots on March 18, 1901 and planned to sell the lots just two days later. Before the sale even started, hundreds of prospective lot owners had built a tent city.

The first stores built in Elk City included general merchandise, grocery stores, lumber, hardware and dry goods. Also springing up were several restaurants, along with the ever present saloons. Professionals included attorneys, physicians and bankers. In Aug, 1901 the Choctaw Railroad was completed and the first train service arrived in town.

By January of the following year, Elk City boasted a population of over 1,000 and more than 60 businesses including two hotels, several boarding houses, a church, two milling companies and two cotton gins. It was also in 1902, that Elk City began to pave its streets with bricks. Though not even a year old yet, the town had already become one of the largest in western Oklahoma.

When Route 66 made her way through town, Elk City responded. In 1931, the US Highway 66 Association held its annual convention in Elk City with more than 20,000 people attending. The event was held at the Casa Grande Hotel, which advertised itself as the only fireproof hotel between Oklahoma City and Amarillo. Today, this historic hotel is home to the Anadarko Basin Museum of Natural History.

When Route 66 was lost to the interstate, Elk City, due to her diversified interests, didn't suffer like so many other cities. In fact, just a few years later the great oil field boom of the early 1980s brought thousands into town, working on the oil rigs. One man who worked the rigs described the city during this time as a "wild west boom town" with 20 men for every woman in the community. Elk City underwent a flurry of building activity and many vintage Route 66 sites were lost. Today, Elk City is called home to a little more than 10,000 people and provides not only a peek at the

Route 66 era, but also that of the Old West at the National Route 66 Museum and Old Town Museum Complex.

Donna and Glen were excited about escaping the interstate

It had been a climb all the way up from Foss to Elk City and onwards, so I was glad of the reprieve down to Sayre. Along the road, I met cyclists Donna and Glen, a couple about my own age, who were travelling east and staying in motels. Donna said that the thought of snakes — real or imagined — was enough to stop her camping out. We chatted, astride our bikes for a few minutes, and they were animated about the ground I would cover in the coming days. They had the expected warnings about water and the wind. There would be long days that I'd anticipated and days when I'd have to ride on the shoulder of the interstate — which I hadn't. Donna spoke of the "dire tyre wire" — the internal wire from truck tyres — that was washed to the sides of the roads. Made of steel, it was particularly unforgiving on bicycle wheels, so thin and fine that it was difficult to find in the tyre after a puncture. All in all, they painted a mixed picture – exhilaration at the scenery, frustration at the road!

Sayre, Oklahoma, got its start in 1901 when the steam engine pushed through. It was primarily dependent upon local livestock and farming. However, this all changed when rich oil and gas fields were found in the area and Sayre began to grow. The Beckham County courthouse, built in 1911, in Sayre, made a thirty-second appearance in the final cut of The Grapes of Wrath. It's a nice little town with many of the old buildings being restored and refurbished. The entire historic downtown district, centred on Main and 4th Streets, was listed on the National Register of Historic Places, as well as the Oklahoma Register, in 2002. It even had, like Chelsea OK, an underpass to keep the residents safe from the original Route 66 traffic.

Jack Rittenhouse, in his 1946 Guidebook To Highway 66, would say of Erick, fourteen miles west of Sayre: "U.S. 66 crosses the one main street of the town, which is the first town you encounter, going west, which has any of the 'true' western look, with its wide, sun baked street, frequent horsemen, occasional sidewalk awning, and similar touches." I was now entering cowboy country and the town really had a "western" feel to it. Unfortunately, many of the buildings lay empty and spoke of better times. With a population of just over a thousand, it had survived, unlike the ghost town of Hext a few miles previous. It had survived with oil and through traffic on Route 66 until the I-40 bypassed it in 1975.

Erick was also the boyhood home of Roger Miller, the late country music legend, Mr. "King of the Road" himself. The stretch of road that enters Erick from Sayre has been renamed Roger Miller Memorial Highway, and that part of Route 66 through town, is called Roger Miller Boulevard. The Roger Miller Museum, which opened in 2004 in a former 1929 café and drugstore building, is on a corner of US 66 (Roger Miller Boulevard). An interviewer once asked Roger Miller where Erick was and Miller replied, "It's close to extinction."

I must confess to being a little excited at the prospect of crossing into Texas – the state line was only eight flat miles out the road. Texola, currently just short of the state line, was born in 1901 and sits near the 100th Meridian. For this reason, the town has been surveyed eight different times over the years and many of its residents have lived in both Oklahoma and Texas, without ever having moved. In its earliest days, the people of the town had a hard time figuring out what to call it, changing the name from Texokla, to Texoma, and Texola. Finally, a town election chose its permanent name when the post office was established in December, 1901. There was no fanfare to the crossing. Texola is home to the Tumbleweed Grill and Waterhole. It sports the sign "There's no other place like this place anywhere near this place so this must be the place." The owner was an artist, who'd moved to the town and seemed like the only occupant of the town. Her paintings were nice, but a bit unwieldy for the bicycle, and the store's stock was a hodge-podge of kitsch. The light beer I got came from a domestic fridge. There wasn't a lot of business being done here.

Still, I appreciated being able to sit out of the heat. In 1940, she said, Texola was called home to over three hundred people. By 1990, it had forty-five, and, today, the number is in the single digits. It was clearly a ghost town, with a lack of business and abandoned buildings. However, the restored Magnolia Service Station, which was listed in the National Register of Historic Places in 1995, causes visitors to stop by and she gets a chance to talk to the world without leaving home.

Looking forward to crossing into Texas in a couple of minutes, I took my leave – only to find that I'd gotten a flat. The holed tyre I'd been using since Tulsa had failed again. I cut a few inches of tubing to make a couple of layers of protection inside the tyre before replacing the tyre. That should hold, but I needed to replace the tyre at the earliest opportunity. Trouble was, there weren't too many cycling options in this neck of the woods – or desert! I might have stopped in Texola – wild camping wouldn't have been a problem with all the abandoned buildings – but I was drawn to the name of Shamrock TX, only another thirteen miles.

Only a fence separated me from the I-40 for the, mostly flat, run to Shamrock, named by an Irish immigrant sheep rancher by the name of George Nickel. In 1890, the Irishman applied to open a post office at his dugout home six miles north of the present town site. Suggesting the name for good luck and courage, the post office never opened because Nickel's home burned down, but the name stuck. Having gained approval for the name, another post office was operated nearby for a short time, but, Shamrock did not get its official beginning until the railway arrived in the summer of 1902.

It was the discovery of oil and the arrival of the Mother Road in 1926 that allowed Shamrock to boom. I was drawn, on arrival, to the Tower Station and U-Drop Inn, in anticipation of a cold beer to round off the day. Representing the art-deco style that was popular in the 1920s and 1930s, the building was completed in 1936. Local newspapers reported it as "the swankiest of swank eating places" and "the most up-to-date edifice of its kind on the U.S. Highway 66 between Oklahoma City and Amarillo." The U-Drop Inn, where "Delicious Food Courteously Served" became the standard, was a welcoming sight to highway travellers and the many buses that pulled in at the diner. Hardly living up to the town's name, I found it was now only a gift shop and no beer was available. I found the Sports Bar, complete with its four patrons and Lacey, the barmaid. Enquiring about a place where I might camp, I was directed to the centre of town, "go right on Main Street and four blocks on your left, there's a campsite". I was surprised that the ACA map didn't have it – until I saw the piece of waste ground on which I could pitch my tent. No toilets, but there was running water. No showers, but I was in town. This mixture of negatives and positives made the $3.00 price tag acceptable.

The minimal price for camping encouraged me to splash out on a steak dinner in Big Vern's Steakhouse beside Chug's Liquor Store. The bike felt jittery without the panniers as I pedalled the few blocks. A couple of beers while waiting and then a lovely steak – I mean, what else would I eat in Texas? The strange accents at a table to my right had me earwigging and then I joined Lee and Thelma, an English couple who were motoring Route 66. We compared experiences, because we'd been travelling the same direction, and, while my opinion was that it was an okay route, with a lot of history, they were blown away by it. It was all they hoped for – and more. But they were both "petrol-heads" who couldn't understand why I'd cycle anywhere. It reinforced my opinion that Route 66 is a driving rather than a cycling experience.

We passed a pleasant hour until nine o'clock, when it became was obvious that the staff wanted to close up and the bar had already been vacated. In a town of less than two thousand souls, the nightlife was always going to be less than scintillating, so we said our goodbyes and "maybe we'll meet down the road" and parted. They were headed for the Holiday Inn Express and I went to my tent.

Day 16 Wed 15 Jun
Campsite to Shamrock TX to Groom TX
Distance 91 kms / 56 miles
Total so Far 1951 kms / 1218.5 miles
Accommodation: $63.95 Chalet Inn, Groom TX

This stretch had little to recommend it. I was travelling across the Texas Panhandle I'd seen in John Wayne, Alan Ladd and Gary Cooper westerns of the fifties and sixties. The place names heard in my youth were beginning to make sense now as I could put them in context. I'd passed south of Cheyenne. While place names in Oklahoma didn't feature much in the movies I'd seen, places in Kansas, Dodge City, Laramie or those connected to the Chisolm cattle trail from Abilene south through Ft Worth and the Cimmaron Route of the Santa Fe Trail were often mentioned. The plain across which I was riding was wide open as far as I could see. A wind blew that gave meaning to the sign I'd seen on a store door, just before crossing from Oklahoma – "Due to strong Oklahoma winds, please hold tightly to the door". Right now, I was lucky to have the wind come from my left rather than into my face. I stopped for a liberal application of sunscreen.

There was nothing in the line of services between Shamrock and McLean so breakfast in McDonalds before leaving stood to me. It was basically a drive-thru' and there hadn't been a soda fountain where I could fill up with iced water as, so I'd had to fill up in the washrooms and had no ice. I still hadn't gotten round to carrying extra water but I found myself reaching for the bottles more than I had been.

McLean had started out as nothing more than a cattle loading site along the Rock Island Railroad, but a large rancher had a vision. Alfred Row, an Englishman, saw greater opportunity for the area and donated land to lay out a town site. Naming the town for W.P. McLean of the Texas Legislature and Railroad Commission, the town had a post office by 1902. A windmill pumped water from a well drilled in the middle of Main Street, and residents hauled their water home in barrels and buckets. In 1912, Alfred Rowe, left McLean to visit his native England. He would never see McLean again. He died on the Titanic when it sank in the Atlantic in the early morning hours of April 15, 1912.

The town prospered even before the arrival of Route 66, becoming a major shipping point for area livestock, gas, and oil, it but through traffic further insured the town's growth for the next several decades. During the Golden Age of Route 66, McLean boasted sixteen service stations, six motels and numerous cafes. Oklahoma based Phillips Petroleum Company built its first Texas service station in McLean in 1927. By 1940 McLean had a population of more than 1,500 with six churches, a newspaper and fifty-nine businesses.

In September of 1942, an area northeast of McLean was chosen to serve as the McLean Permanent Alien Internment Camp during WWII. During its operation, the camp had twenty to thirty buildings and housed three thousand prisoners-of-war. The first were German troops captured in North Africa, who arrived in early 1943. A second group of Germans captured in their Homeland were also retained at the camp. During its time, there were several escape attempts from the camp, but on the bare plains of the Texas panhandle there was nowhere to go. All were recaptured and seemed glad to return to the prison. The camp continued to operate until July 1, 1945.

McLean business owners fought hard to keep McLean alive in the face of other towns' growth. It was obvious that a bypass would draw away the tourist trade which sustained the many service stations, motels and cafes. The town fought to stop, or at least, slow the eventual building of Interstate, but without success. Construction of the bypass started in March of 1982 and was completed in the summer of 1984. Though McLean was the last Texas Route 66 town bypassed by Interstate 40, the move further reduced its population. Today, McLean is called home to just over eight hundred citizens.

Nothing but recreated Gas Stations – but I got my phone back

I almost lost my phone. I'd stopped at a gas station for a cold drink and plugged in the phone to charge. I left without it and only discovered it missing when I stopped to get a picture of the Phillips 66 gas station. Luckily, I hadn't gone far! Reunited, I cracked on towards Alanreed, climbing much of the way. In the distance I saw two cyclists bearing down on me and I pulled over to chat with them. Christopher and Quincey Briscoe were doing the route to Chicago and were interested in my experiences. Christopher was on an electric bike – so he could keep up with his son. They were staying in motels and taking pictures. It wasn't until later that I saw that Christopher is a photographer of significance and, since I met him, had been selected as official photographer for Kirk Douglas' 100th birthday bash. The photographs he took along the route were incredible.

Quincey and Chris Briscoe

I was now aware that I'd soon be cycling on the shoulder of the I-40. I hadn't realised it would be quite so soon, but I might as well get used to the idea. Christopher and Quincey had stayed in the motel in Groom and, hearing that I was bound for that town, recommended "the Grill" for breakfast. They were headed for Shamrock and I recommended Vern's. Perhaps they'd been eating better than me and maybe Vern's might not be as big a deal for them as it had been for me.

There was a Rest Area on the I-40 up ahead that advertised vending machines. It was coming up on lunchtime and I knew I wouldn't make the next eighteen miles without food. Already, I found the heat intense and was amazed that Quincey had chosen to ride in the sun without a shirt. Leaving Shamrock in the morning, I'd been thinking about going on to Conway, but now I realised that I'd be lucky to make Groom. The instant mash with chilli beans added kept me going and I forged on.

By the time I reached the grocery store in Groom, at three-thirty in the afternoon, the temperature was about a hundred degrees and the water bottles I'd replenished at the rest stop had gotten hot. I got two large bottles of Gatorade and a half-gallon of water and asked if I might sit out front to rest. The helpful girl at the cash desk indicated a gazebo across the street where I might get some shade. When I asked if anybody would mind me putting up a small tent there for the night, she reckoned I'd be fine.

Knowing that a Dairy Queen, indicated in the town might be my only food possibility until breakfast, I set off to find it. I was hailed by a lady in the street who wanted to know about my trip. When I said I was going to camp by the gazebo, she said that the town park, between Second and Third Streets, a couple of blocks away, had toilets and, she thought, power. That clinched it for me and I headed off to find it.

I got phone and backup plugged in and charging and unloaded the bike before continuing my search for the Dairy Queen. A "Hunger Buster" combo brought me round and I headed back to the park in good form. The question was whether or not to pitch the tent. The wind was strengthening so a tent might not be the better option. I pulled the panniers under a picnic table to give me a bit of protection from the wind, but it kept getting stronger.

I watched two girls – one on a mobility scooter – navigating the grassy pathway into the park, thinking one was the other's carer. Not at all. They both climbed trees with equal agility. I suppose going for a spin on a mobility scooter is what passes for afternoon excitement in Groom TX. I'd passed a group of three youths on the street, but otherwise, the town might as well have been deserted. I couldn't make myself fully at home until it got towards dark – and a good thing too. The wind seemed as if some supernatural being had exhaled. It continued to get stronger. Unlike the winds in Ireland which normally come in gusts, this one was just one continuous movement of an air mass. Perhaps it was because there are no hills to disrupt it as it blows. The skies darkened and I began to get concerned at the arrival of thick wind-borne dust,. This wasn't something I'd ever experienced, so I felt that, just maybe, it might not be a night for the open air. A siren sounded and I didn't know if it was for a fire or a tornado, so I gathered up my stuff and cycled off to find the motel that Christopher and Quincey had stayed in. I hadn't seen it on the way into town, so it had to be down another street. I could feel my tyre was soft and I reckoned I had a slow flat. Nothing for it but keep going and hope to get under cover before it failed completely.

The motel appeared and I pulled up – only then realising that my stuff was still plugged charging at the park. I was in the process of checking in and asked the guy behind the desk if I could leave my stuff to go back and I'd complete the process on my return. There was no way I was being allowed drop a single bag until I'd handed over the $63.75 for the room. "You pay first." At that stage, all I could think about was my stuff and what a miserable bastard this guy manning the desk of the Chalet Inn was. If I'd had an alternative, I'd have walked away, regardless of the cost.

With my stuff in the room, I made a dash back to the park, recovered my stuff and was buffeted by the wind all the way in both directions. The evening was punctuated by flashes of lightning as I fixed the flat, repairing the puncture rather than committing a fresh tube. I'd another puncture from Texola to mend as well. The news carried and item about Semis being blown over on the I-40 and, since that was my direction of travel, taking a room had been a good idea. The shower made me feel better and a good night's sleep with air-conditioning would prepare me for the intense heat of the coming days.

Day 17 Thu 16 Jun
Groom TX to Amarillo TX
Distance 104 kms / 65 miles
Total so Far 2055 kms / 1283.5 miles
Accommodation: $28.00 KOA Amarillo TX

I'd wanted an early start and had set the alarm for five-fifteen so I'd be at The Grill when it opened at six. The noise in the room caused me to think that the wind was still howling, but, luckily, it was only the air-conditioning. I was glad to get out of the motel. The manager's lack of understanding the previous evening still annoyed me and had left a bad taste. The puncture I'd repaired the evening before had held so I was confident of the tyre lasting the distance to Amarillo. With my gear packed and loaded, I was at the door of The Grill at six – only to find that it didn't open to the public until seven. The owner came along at six-fifteen but said it would take about half an hour to get the grill up and running, but I was welcome to sit inside and wait. While she worked, Karen told me about the town and its history since it was founded in 1903. Although Route 66 passed through and it benefitted from the oil, the population never grew beyond eight hundred people.

Nowadays, the town is home to about five hundred people and survives on passing trade and as a commuter town for Amarillo. She said the big cross caused quite a number of travellers to stop. Located just north of town, the nineteen-story cross, standing 190 feet tall and visible from twenty miles was built in 1995. A Mr. Thomas, disgusted with the huge billboards advertising XXX pornography locations along I-40 wanted to make a public profession of faith along the Interstate. Surrounding the base of the cross are life-sized statues of the 14 Stations of the Cross. Apparently, Groom hasn't been hit by a tornado since. I said that if I'd known that, I might have taken my chances in the public park the previous night and told her of the lack of understanding at the Chalet Inn. I had no problem sharing less than flattering stories, because I share the good stories all the time. I asked about the wind patterns hereabouts and Karen said that, for the next few days, it shouldn't be too bad, but that the heat was going to be severe. I asked if the traffic blockages on the I-40 would divert traffic onto my route and just then a man walked in. "Here's the answer," Karen said. "Al's been out at the scene all night. How's it out there, Al?" It was all clear now. Three semis had been blown over and had to be recovered from the road. The interstate had reopened about four-thirty so traffic was flowing freely again. Karen said it was like the old days, when service stations in town, as well as the local farmers and ranchers, used to do a big business pulling stranded cars out of the infamous Jericho Gap, a stretch of muddy road to the east of Groom. Those travellers not stranded, would breathe a deep sigh of relief if they arrived in town without having fallen prey to the treacherous piece of road.

The Grill omelette was worth waiting for and I thanked Christopher Briscoe, silently, for having recommended it. There are so few real diners left that it's always a pleasure to get home-cooked food along the route. By the time I got back on the road, it was almost eight-thirty, much later than I'd planned. But, luckily, it was going to be a short day – only about forty miles.

The scene of last night's traffic incident was still being cleared up as I passed the scene and wreckers were still recovering two trucks, but at least there was no traffic on my road. Google maps said there was thirty-seven miles to the KOA campsite at Amarillo, so I could easily handle the heat for that distance, although the road rose the whole way.

Going West to East and Buffalo-bound

Pastor Pat was just east of Conway when we met. He was coming from the west and told me what to watch out for between here and Amarillo. He'd wild-camped at a rest stop a few miles back along the interstate and had been worried that his tent wouldn't survive the wind of last night. It had, but he hadn't had a whole lot of sleep and felt sluggish this morning. He was bound for Chicago and would, he said, continue to his home in Buffalo, NY. He'd been listening to other people's problems for fifteen years and said he'd felt the need to take time out to reflect on his own for a change. He would take a break in Tulsa to visit his son and his wife and daughter would come out to join him for the week off the bike. I remembered Graham, whom I met in the bike shop in Newton KS in 2014. His daughter had come to visit him for a week and by the time I met him, he said he was having a lot of trouble motivating himself to get back on the bike. It's hard to know if breaks along the way, to spend time with people who don't actually know about the cycle, is that much of a good idea. I'd have to give that thought consideration in the next few days in regard to Patty Lyman's invitation to stop off and go to Blanding UT.

At the rest area a few miles on, I stopped to fill my water bottles and was approached by Ted. He was taking his family – wife, two daughters, one son and three dogs – to visit the Grand Canyon. They were at a picnic table close to mine and waved when I looked over at them. Ted wanted me to join them for food. I didn't want to intrude and said I'd be getting back on the road soon, but he insisted and the family made room for me and I tucked into homemade sandwiches and a bottle of Gatorade from the cooler. It was great. Ted was a cyclist but hadn't done big distances yet. They hailed from Austin TX, and, when I mentioned Lance Armstrong, Ted said that the US had been let down by him. He said he still had difficulty getting his head around Armstrong's doping and said it was almost as if the lie was preferable to the truth. I said I knew how he felt – we all need heroes and to have that image shattered is something that hurts.

I took a longer break than I'd anticipated, but eventually got on the road with their good wishes following me. I must have been strong after the rest because, although the road was a succession of straight-as-a-die sections, I made good progress and arrived at the KOA campsite at eleven-thirty. I'd probably put more effort into the ride, knowing I was having a short day.

Once I'd pitched the tent and gotten my gear unloaded, I asked the girl on the desk if she knew of a bicycle shop locally. She did – and said they might even deliver what I needed. Excellent news, but my happiness didn't last. They were shorthanded today and couldn't deliver. They had what I needed – tyre, tubes, gloves and pump – but I'd have to come in. That was another twelve miles each-way, a distance I hadn't bargained on. I'd been hoping to chill out, and, maybe do a little sightseeing in the afternoon. Instead, I was going to be competing with traffic again.

On the positive side, I covered the ground quickly with the bike stripped down and a mechanic in the bike shop fitted the new tyre and checked the tension in the spokes on front and back wheels. I felt confident heading back into Historic Downtown to see how Route 66 was remembered before going to the campsite. Land prices were never a consideration in the building of this town. Amarillo in Spanish means "yellow" and the town took its name from the colour of the clay in the area. 6th Ave SW was wide, long and shadeless. Mexican influence was pronounced with the number of restaurants and diners. Stores sold cowboy stuff and Route 66 souvenirs. There was nothing that would have caused me to part with money, but I did stop for a beer at Wild Bill's. The rest and the cold beer set me up for the return journey and I felt good.

Texas does it – clearly

At the campsite, the girl at the desk asked if I'd gotten sorted and said that the Big Texan, a famous bar and restaurant – a "must-see" on Route 66 – operated a courtesy bus from the campsite. She said it would collect me from my tent site and would drop me back there whenever I wanted to return. Since I needed to eat anyway, I decided to avail of it. There was too much wind and dust to consider breaking out the Trangia. I had just enough time for a shower and a change of clothes before the next shuttle left. Purcell was the driver and I shared with another family of parents and two kids.

The Big Texan is a themed bar and restaurant opened in the late fifties when Bob Lee went seeking a large steak in the midst of "cow country." To his surprise, Amarillo sported not a single cowboy steak house, which Lee soon began to rectify. The Big Texan Steak Ranch opened, claiming to serve the largest steak in Texas. But simply serving the largest steak wasn't enough. The story goes that cowboys from across the area came to the Big Texan for a good steak, and Bob had noticed more than once that everyone enjoyed the friendly carnivorous competition between the cowboys. One Friday night, Bob pulled the local guys together to see who could eat the most. He charged them five dollars apiece to participate with the pot awarded to the winner at the end of the contest. The rules were simple: don't leave the table until you're finished, and if you lost your dinner you lost the contest. But while Bob was rounding up travellers, he didn't for a minute overlook the local ranch hands, cowboys and characters whose work and lives he was turning into a legend.

After quickly devouring a couple of steaks, one hungry hand asked for a salad and a shrimp cocktail. A couple of steaks later, he asked for a baked potato and a dinner roll. After eating those sides, he asked for his fifth, one-pound steak. When the cowboy finished, he had consumed 72-oz. of good Texas beef along with the rest of the dinner. Bob vowed that night that anyone else who could match that limit would get his or her dinner free. Lee soon began promoting a Free 72 ounce Steak Dinner if customers could eat the whole thing in less than an hour. It wasn't long before the promotion gained national attention and travellers thinking of

Amarillo, immediately associated it with the Texan Steak Ranch, making the restaurant a "must stop" for travellers of the Mother Road.

When I-40 came through Amarillo, bypassing Route 66, Lee moved the restaurant nearer the traffic, but the famous steakhouse retained its reputation as a Mother Road landmark. In addition to its more than forty-year steak promotion and seating for four hundred and fifty in its restaurant, the Big Texan sports a motel, Old West entertainment, a gift shop, and even a Horse Hotel, all decorated to resemble an Old West town.

Paul and Rick

Because I was on my own, I wanted a spot at the counter and two men made space for me between them. It was a most relaxing and enjoyable few hours. Both were ex-military and travelling separately. Paul was from Galveston where he lived with his dog. He said that, having the RV outside his door meant that whenever there was a threat of a storm – Galveston is very low-lying – he could "fuel up and bug out". He heads out to State Parks to volunteer for the summer and would be heading off to Lubbock the next day. Mention of that town brought us to a famous son of there – Buddy Holly. That was the way the night went. Rick was from Roswell NM and brought us up-to-date on the aliens of that location. I said I had a beer called "Alien" from that neck of the woods in 2014, and had been impressed. No wonder aliens had chosen the area. The conversation flowed with the beer and Rick told of his adventures visiting Ireland some years previously. He'd covered a lot of ground and hoped to go back again. Right now, he was going on to Dallas to meet with his son on Father's Day. We, all three, got on well together.

Keith, in Chandler, had warned me off the Big Texan, saying it was a rip-off. I suppose, to someone on a tight budget, my spending there would have appeared an unwarranted extravagance, but, in truth, the steak, onion rings green beans and baked potato was excellent and the company great. The Texas Red Amber Ale was lovely, served in ice-cold two-pint glasses. I had two. I asked about the Tony Christie song "Is this the way to Amarillo". It had been in my head like an earworm since I'd seen the place on my map. Nobody there had heard of it and I came to the conclusion that as many people knew "the way to Amarillo" as there were in Athenry who knew where the "Fields" were. It was a great night and, again, I realised how important social interaction was to me. On the other hand, because I felt so good after being in company, perhaps the "hit" was all the better for its lack of frequency.

I finished up and went outside, where a cowboy called a limo that brought me back to my tent. I was a happy camper as I got into bed. Perhaps it is a measure of how lonely solo travelling can be from time to time that I was so happy to have spent the evening in company.

Day 18 Fri 17 Jun
Amarillo TX to Adrian TX
Distance 94 kms / 59 miles
Total so Far 2149 kms / 1342.5 miles
Accommodation: Free in RV Park, Adrian TX

Amarillo was so big that the Historic Route 66 area I'd seen was almost lost in the city. I wondered how it was that two centres of population – Groom and Amarillo – both founded about the same time, should have developed so differently over the years. Amarillo had a population of almost two hundred thousand, a well-developed industrial base, a major military presence and a significant railroad infrastructure, while Groom struggled to retain its population of about five hundred. Amarillo is about halfway across the Texas Panhandle and, long before Route 66, was a major agricultural centre in cattle country.

I made reasonable progress once I got on the road just after bright. McDonalds provided breakfast after eleven miles, still only on the western outskirts of the city. The benefit was that I always imagine miles drop away when I'm pedalling in a built-up area. The shoulder was fine and drivers courteous. This city might have begun with horses but, now, was most definitely, given over to cars. My stop allowed me to give my phone a bit of a charge while I ate and kept an eye on the bike. I'd found that, since leaving Illinois and Missouri, the towns through which Route 66 travelled – especially the bigger ones – had a history that predated the route and, so, the impact didn't seem to have been so great. Or maybe it was that the more contemporary history of automotive heritage wasn't as significant as that of cattle in this region.

Just outside the western edges of the city, I rejoined the northern frontage road of I-40. I would be either on this road or beside it for the foreseeable future, so I might as well get used to it. I could see across the two frontage roads and the interstate, the entrance to the Cadillac Ranch, an iconic attraction on Route 66. Several myths exist about its origin, the most popular of which is the story told of an eccentric Amarillo, Texas millionaire would buy one Cadillac after another and when it was time to buy a new one, he would have the old one buried nose first on his land. However, the truth is, the Cadillac Ranch was a planned artistic endeavour.

Texas millionaire Stanley Marsh 3 was an eccentric. He was also said to be very down to earth, quickly disregarding the "III" as too pretentious and using "3" instead. In 1973, Marsh invited a San Francisco artists' collective called the Ant Farm to help him in the creation of a unique work of art for his sprawling ranch just west of Amarillo. The group set about acquiring ten used Cadillac's, ranging in model years from 1948 to 1963. Built along Route 66, the cars were meant to represent the "Golden Age" of American automobiles. Most of the cars were purchased from junk yards and were then buried nose-down, facing west along the old highway. Those that could run, were driven into the half-burial holes, the rest were hoisted in.

The project was completed in 1974 and, for a while, the cars displayed their original paint jobs – turquoise, banana yellow, gold, and sky blue. The monument was barely opened, when people were scratching or painting their names in the cars. Over time, vandals and souvenir hounds smashed the windows, made off with all the chrome, radios, speakers and even some of the doors. The wheels have since been welded to the axles to prevent more theft. However, Marsh said "We think it looks better every year." Visitors came from all over the world, leaving their mark on the ever-thickening graffiti covered cars. Throughout the years, the Cadillac Ranch has been repainted many times. In May, 2002, the cars were restored to their original colours. In June, 2003 the cars were again painted, this time in flat black, in response to the passing of the founding member of the Ant Farm. The monument was built as a public sculpture and visitors are encouraged to participate in it. So, it's ok if you take your can of paint with you, leaving your name or an inspiring message, which will, no doubt, be erased by another message soon.

Crossing the interstate without doubling back for a few miles wasn't an option, so I couldn't get a close-up photograph. I don't do "doubling back" and was content to lean the bike against a fence and observe the constant flow of visitors approaching and leaving the site. I felt it was like driving past Newgrange Passage Tomb in County Meath – you can see the structure but, intuitively, you know you're missing something by not visiting the site. It's a trade-off.

During the dustbowl days of the late 1920s and early 1930s, Wildorado suffered along with the rest of the Midwest as crops were ruined by drought and many a pioneer gave up and headed West to escape the blinding dust storms. Along with numerous refugees from Oklahoma, these desperate folks loaded up their belongings seeking a better life and headed down the newly founded Route 66.

To make matters worse during this time, the state bank, the grain elevator, and the mercantile store were robbed and burglarized several times by even more desperate men from nearby Borger, Texas. It got so bad that on January 29, 1928, it made national headlines when the Syracuse Herald in New York ran a headline stating: "Wildorado – Texas Town Plundered So Many Times That Six Shooters No Longer Terrorize." The articled continued to say that the Wildorado State Bank "has been robbed eight times in the last three years, and the general store next door has been visited by bandits so frequently that the proprietors have lost count of the number of times they have looked down revolver barrels."

Wilderado's Windy Cow Café was a clue to the standing of cattle in this region. It was a welcome sight as I was in need of the services and, answering calls of nature aren't easy in full view of America passing by on the interstate. I relaxed and read another few pages of "The Grapes of Wrath" – keeping pace with the movement of the Joads across Texas "Two days the families were in flight, but on the third the land was too huge for them and they settled into a new technique of living; the highway became their home and movement their medium of expression." I had also read Jack Kerouac's seminal novel, "On the Road" and felt that the frantic nature of his "beat" movement was just too incomprehensible for me. Steinbeck put the Joads in the transport of its time – a God-fearing family trying to survive and help each other, whereas Kerouac's heroes were of a different order – focusing on expression, freedom, rebellion and escape. They struck a note with late fifties younger generation trying to find its place in post-war America and deciding that it would be a New Age. They would assert their identity through experimentation with drugs, and through contravention of existing values and strictures. No wonder it was such a bestseller. But Kerouac went too quickly for me. Steinbeck sent his characters on an odyssey and I was sitting in a town his family laboured through – "The land rolled by like great stationary ground swells. Wildorado and Vega and Boise and Glenrio. That's the end of Texas."

I couldn't delay any longer. The temperature was rising and the morning was progressing. A flat twelve miles brought me to Vega and away from the smell of the stockyard in Wildorado. The wind was in my face – just to advise me that the lack of a hill did not mean an absence of punishment. My proposed stop for the day was Adrian – exactly halfway on Route 66 – and it didn't promise much in the way of supplies, so I stopped for lunch at the Dairy Queen. I was becoming accustomed to chicken strips, fries and a refillable coke at or about midday. Free refills always swung it for me and I was glad to get out of the heat and the wind-borne dust.

Halfway into the "forest"

It was just four in the afternoon when I rolled up to the halfway marker in Adrian TX. While a girl with a family name Ryan took my picture in front of the marker, showing 1139 miles in either direction – I knew my mileage was higher because the Adventure Cycling Association had rerouted cyclists away from traffic when appropriate – the Midpoint Café was just closing. Seemed a little early and I was hot and bothered. Fran Houser, in the Sunflower Station next door, was a Godsend. She gave me bottles of cold water and showed me where the garden hose was, in case I wanted to replenish my bottles. She had been the owner of the Midpoint Café until she'd sold it to the current owners and was as perplexed as I was that they insisted in shutting up shop at four. I wondered where I might camp for the night and ventured that there must be little difficulty with stealth-camping in the area. Fran said that her friend, Bud, ran the RV Park for his boss and would have no difficulty in letting me stay there. She'd give him a call. Fran was always going to be helpful – it was only later that I discovered that she'd been the inspiration for Flo, a character in the Pixar movie, Cars.

She watered her plants and went home, leaving me to sit and charge my phone in shelter from the hot afternoon sun. I was finished for the day and in no hurry anywhere. I made contact with Bud at the RV Park. In a stroke of good fortune, it turned out that he was taking care of his boss's pedigree show cattle that evening and brought me along with him in his truck to the farm a few miles outside town. It gave me a chance to look at the countryside without the pressure of cycling at the same time. Bud had the most wonderful accent and I could have listened to him all night. He really seemed so laid back that each word seemed a conscious effort. I suppose when you live in a place where everything happens slowly, there's no need to rush even your speech. He'd been away from Adrian for many years and only came back to look after a relative. Now he managed the RV Park and said that he'd no problem if I wanted to sleep in the office rather than pitch the tent outside.

We reached the farm and the three animals Bud had responsibility for were in their pens. They lived in the lap of luxury with shade and air-conditioning and big fans during the day. These were show animals and were treated a bit like thoroughbreds in a Kildare stud farm. At night they were released into the paddock for exercise and feeding. On the way back, I pointed out the wind turbines and Bud said there was about one for every two inhabitants of Adrian. While they'd been constructed, Bud had been retained for their security and it had given him a great opportunity to get out into the wilderness of the area and see what rural Texas Panhandle had to offer in terms of flora and fauna through the four seasons. "It might look like a desert," he said, "but nothing could be further from the truth. Those who know the Burren in County Clare would be of the same opinion!

We went back to Adrian, via the road I'd be taking in the morning. This would allow me avoid the interstate for a couple of miles beyond Gruhlkey. Any little comfort was to be welcomed. Bud's office was air-conditioned and I'd considered camping so as not to be a hindrance to anyone coming and going, but once we'd appreciated the spectacular sunset and made it back to the RV Park after nightfall, it was obvious that we were in for a windy night. Dust was being swept across the ground and the light on the front of the office was motion-sensitive. It might keep me awake so I accepted Bud's of shelter.

I prepared my dinner and, by the light of the office, I looked at the next series of maps. There's always a sense of wonder at the unpacking of the new maps. Although I'd made myself familiar with them all, long before this trip had begun, my interest had always been in the immediate future rather than a few days down the road. A long-range plan on this trip was about twelve hours – a day's pedalling! I was past the stage of wondering why the hell I was doing this. It had been something I'd had to work through in 2014 – was it to prove something? Was it adventure? Was it to inspire? Or was I just crazy? It was a little of all of these reasons and once I figured that out, I didn't have to justify it to anyone – even to myself. If the mileage from here was the mileage I'd cycle from here to the west coast, I was halfway into the "forest", and from here I was heading out the other side. It was a good feeling as I settled down to sleep.

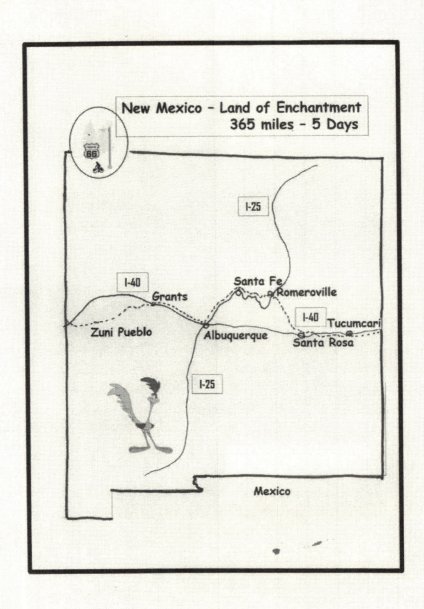

Chapter 6

New Mexico – Land of Enchantment

Day 19 Sat 18 Jun
Adrian TX to Tucumcari NM
Distance 104 kms / 65 miles
Total so Far 2253 kms / 1407.5 miles
Accommodation: Free in Ben's Home, Clovis NM

In June 2014, while on my TransAm route and travelling with Henry and Danielle, Laura and Noah, I met Ben in Cedar City. He'd been stranded there with a broken pedal and was waiting for a replacement to be sent from his home in Clovis, NM. He'd subsequently joined our little chain gang and I travelled with him until the Colorado/Kansas Stateline. His parents, Carol and Ed, had hosted us in the KOA Campsite north of Pueblo, CO and, when I'd said goodbye, it appeared that any further contact would only be through Facebook. Ben and Laura had teamed up and had gone to Vermont at the end of the cycle and I never expected to meet with them again. Ben had subsequently moved back to Clovis and was starting his own business there. I'd made contact when this trip had firmed up and, while Carol and Ed would be in California as I passed through, they welcomed me to come and spend time in Clovis.

There was little to pack up and, once the alarm sounded at five-fifteen, I got it done while the water was heating for porridge. I even treated myself to a Swiss Miss chocolate drink to get me going. I wouldn't feel the need to stop for breakfast. I stopped at Fran's store to fill the water bottles.

When the frontage road ran out, I had to get on the I-40 and deal with the traffic. I was glad of the hi-vis vest as I trundled along the shoulder with the sound of trucks, RVs and cars too close for comfort. Still, it was mostly downhill for the next twenty miles and, as luck would have it, the wind was mostly at my back while the sky was overcast. All in all, it was a perfect day for pedalling.

Straddling the border between Texas and New Mexico is the ghost town of Glenrio. Once a monument along the boom and bust highway of Route 66, now it remains home only to the animals and blowing tumbleweeds of the prairie. The name Glenrio stems from the Scottish word for "valley" and the Spanish word for river and it is neither in a valley nor along a river.

A post office was first established on the New Mexico side of the community, but, the mail arrived at the railroad depot located on the Texas side. Glenrio became the subject of a long battle between both states for tax rights, by virtue of its precarious location crossing Texas and New Mexico. By 1920, it had a hotel, a hardware store, and a land office, as well as several grocery stores, service stations, and cafes. There were no bars on the Texas side of the community, since Deaf Smith County was dry, and no service stations on the New Mexico side because of that state's higher gasoline tax. In 1938, just months after the final pavement through this terrain of Route 66 was finished, John Steinbeck's The Grapes of Wrath was filmed in Glenrio for three weeks.

I was passing through, anxious only to cross the state line and pick up one more state, but I paused to reflect, in a desolate Glenrio, whose old main street still stands intact, on how small places in Ireland might easily fall to abandonment unless a viable vision is developed for their survival. These deserted villages already exist as famine villages – but a new wave might well join them unless a reason exists for their survival. Politicians, particularly those representing rural West of Ireland constituencies should be forced to look at these ghost towns as a wake-up call. Viable towns had prospered from being linked by the original Route 66 – only to be killed off by the interstate.

I crossed under the sign, Welcome to New Mexico – Land of Enchantment, the forty-seventh state of the United States, and immediately pulled off the road into the Glenrio Visitor Centre, where I was offered a free cup of coffee. It was palatable too, so, already New Mexico had won me over. A peanut bar from a vending machine rounded off the break. There were facts and figures available for the state but what jumped out at me, unsurprisingly, was that it only became a state in 1912 and had the second highest population after Alaska, by percentage, of Native Americans. It had seen four hundred years of Spanish settlement and those influences, in everything about the state, would become more and more apparent.

Back on the frontage road, I was protected from the traffic – even if nothing could offer protection from the sun, which had appeared with a vengeance. I still had assistance from a tailwind for the twenty miles to San Jon, where I took a bit of a meal break. The Taste of India was not exactly what I was looking for and I settled for chicken strips and fries to keep me going for the last twenty miles to Tucumcari. It seemed that settlements seemed to have occurred every twenty miles – almost as that was the limit of travel of an individual in a day. The last miles were easy and I pedalled down the wide road into Tucumcari, a sizeable place with a population of over five thousand people. It seemed particularly quiet, so it must have been siesta time. In need of shade so I could call Ben, I pulled in under a canopy outside what I believed to be a store. I asked for a Coke and the lady refused to take money from me. It was some kind of community centre and she said she was glad to welcome me to town.

Ben said he'd leave Clovis immediately and I should see him in about an hour. I said I wouldn't be off the main drag and he should keep an eye out for the bike. I'd be inside – probably in a bar! La Cita on Main Street seemed like a good place but didn't serve beer. The girl there sent me on down the street to where her sister had a place and I found the Pow Wow

Restaurant. I texted Ben and settled down with a beer. The longer I sat, the more I felt I should check out the menu. I ordered the beef quesadillas and waited. A man approached me and asked about my trip. We spoke briefly and he left. My meal arrived and the girl said it had been paid for. She said I'd been speaking with the owner.

Fantastic to meet up with Ben again

We had a great reunion when Ben arrived and caught up over a Bud Light before loading the bike into the truck and setting off for Clovis. I could relax and chat my way through the almost-desert landscape until we arrived at Ben's home, where I met his brother Marshall, another acquaintance from 2014. Ben was probably delighted to get home since, starved of conversation, I hadn't shut up since I got in the truck!

I showered, changed and sat to chat again, asking Ben about his move back home, his business and about Laura. Time flew and at six-thirty we three went to a Mexican restaurant in town, where the food was good and reasonable. By nine-thirty, I was only ready for sleep and we decided on a plan of action for the following day. Ben would drop me to Santa Rosa instead of Tucumcari and save me sixty miles – a day's pedalling. I would find a campsite there and rest up for the remainder of the day. That would have me up and running the next day as I prepared to tackle the hills of New Mexico. There had been no point in asking Ben about elevations – he was an incredible climber – but he said he felt they wouldn't cause me difficulty.

Day 20 Sun 19 Jun
Clovis NM to Santa Rosa NM
Distance 0 kms / 0 miles
Total so Far 2253 kms / 1407.5 miles
Accommodation: €19.95, Santa Rosa Campground / RV Park

Woke at six, called home at seven and brought my journal up to date. I'd been poring over the map when Ben got up about eight. Getting him to drive me to Santa Rosa wouldn't be putting that much extra on him and, when we left at ten, it seemed a shorter journey than from Tucumcari. I'd seen the RV Park on the map – one of three listed camping options, which made me think I was in a tourist location – and we found it. We checked for vacancies before going for food.

I paid my fee and could take my pick of sites. There was the usual – laundry, showers and washrooms – but it also had a restaurant and pool. Once we unloaded my stuff and we said our goodbyes, Ben headed for home and I faced into a full day of idleness. With no indication of high winds or storms, I felt the tent would benefit from an airing, so I set up without the flysheet.

My pre-tour planning had me in Santa Rosa on Fri 24 Jun and here I was – a week ahead of schedule. I'd spoken to Ben about my dilemma in regard to pace. His opinion was that, if I was comfortable with the pace, I should carry on until I was closer the end and then slow down and smell the flowers. The truth was that I hadn't really suffered at all on this trip. I'd been fitter starting and the terrain was flatter. My planning had been based on the misery of 2014. I was learning all the time. Of more immediate concern were wildfires which were burning south of Albuquerque in the Gila National Forest. They should be far enough away not to impede my progress, but the nature of these things is that the weather might change, new fires might erupt or the existing one might spread. Ben was probably right. I should keep going while the going was good. I set the alarm for quarter-past four in the morning – and thought it might not be early enough.

Day 21 Mon 20 Jun
Santa Rosa NM to Romeroville NM
Distance 100 kms /62.50 miles
Total so Far 2353 kms / 1470 miles
Accommodation: €27.50 KOA Campground

The map indicated "very limited services next 96 miles". Okay, this was the adventure I'd been looking for. There's an, apparently, ancient Chinese curse "Be careful what you wish for," and I was going to face a number of issues. The prevailing wind would be in my face, the road would rise all the way and I would be riding across desert. I felt a sense of insecurity and realised, not for the first time, that I was alone in this endeavour. Nobody was going to help me and if I wanted to progress, I had to do it myself. It's a bit like sitting on the bank of a river where the bridge is gone – either settle down there, or figure out how to cross.

I got an extra water bottle before setting off and was on the road at five, fuelled by oatmeal and hot chocolate, and benefitting from a wonderful downhill start to the day. However, what goes down in New Mexico, most certainly has to go up. My map took me through Santa Fe, state capital of New Mexico, although Route 66 follows I-40 from Santa Rosa to

Albuquerque. In its early days, Route 66 went through the state capital following the Old Pecos Trail from Santa Rosa. The path wound through Dilia, Romeroville and Pecos on its way to Santa Fe. Beyond the capital, the Mother Road continued on a particularly nasty stretch down La Bajada Hill toward Albuquerque. One of the most challenging sections of Route 66, the five hundred-foot drop along narrow switch backs struck terror in the hearts of many early travellers, so much so that locals were often hired to drive vehicles down the steep slope. Although plans were that Santa Fe would continue to stay on the route of the Mother Road, it was not to be, due to political manoeuvrings of the New Mexico Governor in 1937.

Governor Hannett blamed the Santa Fe politicians for his failing to be re-elected and, vowing to get even, he rerouted the highway in his last few months as governor. The road was built so hastily that it was forced through both public and private lands without benefit of official right-of-ways and, by the time the new governor was in place, a new highway connected Route 66 from Santa Rosa to Albuquerque, bypassing the capital city and its many businesses. The new route was more direct and reduced some of the more treacherous road conditions and I-40 would follow this path many years later.

All in all, there seemed to be enough excitement in store for me over the next few days. Once I crossed the Pecos River, a memory from westerns of my youth – whether it was Zane Grey's West of the Pecos or as a sign of general lawlessness. The blurb for the TV series, Judge Roy Bean referred to it as "the wildest spot in the United States ... virtually beyond the reach of the authorities, the railroads, then pushing their way west, attracted the most vicious characters in the country. It was said that all civilization and law stopped at the east bank of the Pecos. It took one man, a lone storekeeper who was sick of the lawlessness, to change all this. His name was Judge Roy Bean." He became the only law west of the Pecos River. I was climbing hard. I entered the I-40 and kept my head down as I pushed along the shoulder gaining one thousand feet in the first few miles as I got out of the river bed. It was a clear demonstration of how extensive the river had once been.

At Exit 263, I left I-40, heading north on Hwy 84. From the look of the map, the gas station at Dilia had shown promise but failed to deliver in reality. I'd put in thirty miles without a coffee or soda stop and I'd just crossed the Pecos River again. The two water bottles were emptied once the sun came out properly at eight and I replenished them from the hydration pack I'd stowed under the stuff on the back rack. Note to self: find space for more water.

Chasing shadows

Hunger set in and began to preoccupy me. This was a desert and I was alone. I hadn't seen a car for some time. The only centre of population marked on the map was Los Montoyas – not big enough to have a population recorded – a further fifteen miles from Dilia. There was nothing for it but to keep going. By this time, I'd well-learnt from my trip across Nevada in 2014 – keep applying the sunscreen.

The road stretched out in front. The good shoulder, littered with debris, designed to flatten my tyres, was of no benefit. I cycled on the main lane without worry – there were few cars. Google Maps refers to Los Montoyas as Apache Springs and it certainly looked like Indian Country. At a crossroads, I thought of taking shelter at what looked like a deserted building, but it was all sealed up. The scrub offered no protection and I worried a little. If I didn't get food soon, I wouldn't be able to cycle – and stopping out here was not really an option. An open gate on the right led to a building that appeared from the architecture to be either a church or the home of a devout person. Nothing ventured, nothing gained so I took myself up the hill to where a woman was working at the back of the building. I asked if I might shelter for a while and she had no problem – even throwing in two bottles of cool, if not cold, water.

Her husband arrived and helped her tidy up the area. They'd had mass on Thursday, something they have every third Thursday, celebrated by the priest from Las Vegas, twenty miles away. They left and I continued with food preparations – boiling water to add to my dehydrated pasta and chicken meal. This was to have been my main meal of the day, but I needed it now, not later. A chocolate drink and a rest – an hour of shuteye passed in a blink – and I got back on the road, feeling strong even though the heat was at its worst. I didn't have far to go – about eight miles to Romeroville, but if I'd not eaten, hunger and heat could have taken a severe toll.

There was a slight downhill for the last few hundred yards to the gas station on I-25. It was a welcome sight and a large Coke was first on the agenda – followed by a refill.

I met Steve and Sherry from Albuquerque, just returning home from a "Ride the Rockies" cycling event, who insisted in giving me landline and cellphone numbers in case I ran into trouble in Albuquerque. They also warned me to mind my bike there. I was too exhausted to be properly sociable and sitting in the sun didn't help my mood. I was glad the day was over and all I would have to do was cover the last mile, back across the interstate to the KOA Las Vegas Campsite. As I sat there, Steve returned and gave me an AAA map of New Mexico and Arizona. This was a wonderful gift. A larger scale than my map of the overall USA would save me unfolding that one every time I wanted to get information about the wider area. Following the ACA maps slavishly, one would never realise that the leg to Santa Fe was not really necessary if the object was to get straight to the west coast. Looking at the route on this new map gave me a much clearer picture.

Being first to book in at the KOA in the early afternoon, I got my choice of pitches. I chose the shaded one and got change for the laundry. I settled down to wait for evening, glad the day was over.

Day 22 Tue 21 Jun
Romeroville NM to Madrid NM
Distance 149 kms /93 miles
Total so Far 2502 kms / 1563 miles
Accommodation: Free: Ballpark

The trouble with getting on the bike at four-fifteen in the morning, to avoid some of the day's heat, is that there's nowhere open for breakfast. I was on the frontage road of I-25, a connection with my trip of 2014. The odd-numbered interstates are north-south and the even-numbered are east-west. In 2014, it was at the KOA on I-25 in Pueblo, that I'd stayed with Ben's parents for a rest day.

I filed this away and concentrated on the job at hand. Forty miles into the day, I reached Pecos and stopped for a breakfast of Omelette with toast before tackling the climb of the day. Glorieta, at over seven and a half thousand feet was not to be sneezed at. The Santa Fe Trail National

Scenic Byway I was following, commemorates the Santa Fe Trail, a 19th-century transportation route through central North America connecting Independence, Missouri with Santa Fe, New Mexico. It had served as a vital commercial highway until the introduction of the railroad to Santa Fe in 1880. Trade from Mexico City had been carried along the Camino Real de Tierra Adentro to Santa Fe until then. I'd previously crossed the Santa Fe Trail in 2014 at Alexander KS, five hundred miles to the northeast.

The Comanches, across whose territory the trail passed, demanded compensation for granting passage and this represented another market for American traders. Comanche raiding farther south in Mexico isolated New Mexico, making it more dependent on the American trade, and provided the Comanches with a steady supply of horses for sale. By the 1840s, trail traffic along the Arkansas Valley was so heavy that bison herds could not reach important seasonal grazing land and this contributed to their collapse, in turn hastening the decline of Comanche power in the region.

The Trail was used as the 1846 U.S. invasion route of New Mexico during the Mexican–American War. After the U.S. acquisition of the Southwest ending that conflict, the trail helped open the region to U.S. economic development and settlement, playing a vital role in the expansion of the U.S. into the lands it had acquired. This was a lot of information to take in while eating breakfast and avoiding the elephant in the room that was the upcoming climb.

Glorieta was the scene of a battle during the American Civil War, often referred to as the Gettysburg of the West. The Union Forces' victory here stopped The Confederate strategy to seize Fort Union northeast of Santa Fe. Colorado and California would have been next to fall, if it had been successful. It could have been a different history, had the Union forces not prevailed.

Getting over this hill would open up the road to Santa Fe for me. It's not normally allowed to ride a bicycle on the interstate, but, where no frontage road – an alternative – exists, it's permitted. Here in New Mexico, road-building seemed to have been minimal and I had to share the interstate with slow-moving trucks uphill to the pass at 7,432ft. After that, I was motoring downhill to Canoncito and off the interstate to the Old Las Vegas Hwy where I paid a visit to a bike shop. Spin Doc was a well-appointed store and I thought I'd get a patch for the tyre I was carrying. It had barely been broken in before it suffered from a nail in Tulsa. With the patch in my pocket – the girl in the shop seemed to know exactly what I needed – I headed off on the last ten miles to Santa Fe. It was only later that I saw she had sold me a puncture repair kit – as if I didn't have enough of them.

The city was impressive. The low-rise architecture made an effort to retain the colonial style. Founded in 1610, Santa Fe is the oldest state capital in the United States. I found it to be a comfortable place that would have attracted me enough to consider putting down roots for a day or two, if I hadn't been travelling alone. I didn't have the issues that Steinbeck gave the Joad family, when he caused their truck to break down on this stretch between Santa Rosa and Albuquerque.

I stopped off at a café for a sandwich which actually had fresh salad in it – the first I'd seen since Chicago. It immediately created the right impression for me. This was a good town. I called into the REI Store on Market St for a few more packed meals, before carrying on – only as far as Second Street Brewery at The Railyard, two hundred yards away, where I sat among all the younger people having a well-deserved beer. I had two options – I could stay here, where there were bike shops, hostels and restaurants with what seemed to be a great lifestyle, or I could carry on a further thirty miles to Madrid. Of course I took the latter option. Loneliness in a crowd is worse than solitude.

The fact that it was generally downhill to Madrid was a major factor in my decision to go on. The route shifted onto the Turquoise Trail, a scenic by-way linking Santa Fe and Albuquerque and it brought me out of town along a cycle trail before depositing me on a quiet road going all the way to Madrid – downhill for fifteen miles followed by a three-mile uphill slog to The Old Boarding House Mercantile. Madrid had an odd feel to it. I could only buy water by the half-gallon and I sat outside on the veranda rehydrating. Three others – and judging by their conversation – not troubled by employment, sat at a neighbouring table. Deciding that I'd better find somewhere to camp, I got back on the bike. A girl from across the road called to me and said I should consider staying at the Ballpark – "just pick the quiet corner, furthest from town." Nobody would mind. I'd seen it on my way into town, but thought it might be just a little cheeky. In 2014, it would have been the automatic thing to do – camp on city property – but that was on a different route.

With my tent erected behind some billboards, I set about checking out the town. Listed as having a population of just over two hundred, this place is obviously a favourite with day-trippers from Santa Fe. Its artisan shops and galleries gave it a kind of hippie feeling. At the end of a line of gift shops, I found the Mine Shaft Tavern, where I went for a burger. The kitchen had closed – it was seven o'clock – so I went across the road where I got wings and a pint.

Madrid's history is colourful, beginning in the early 1800's when squatters arrived and mined coal in the area. Santa Fe railroad brought a spur to Madrid in 1892 to exploit this important resource and, according to the Mine Shaft Tavern, over three thousand people lived and worked in Madrid, which sat on thirty square miles of hard and soft coal.

At its peak the town produced 250,000 tons of coal a year and had boasted a population exceeding Albuquerque. Oscar Huber, who worked for the coal company, and gained controlling interest after the original owner

George Caseman was killed in a drilling accident in 1936, provided well for Madrid. Residents enjoyed a hospital, paved streets and unlimited electricity in their homes. The Mineshaft Tavern which burned to the ground on Christmas Day 1944, was rebuilt. The pine and oak bar is still known as the "longest bar in the state." Huber also built the first illuminated baseball park west of the Mississippi. The lights were turned on in 1922 putting Madrid in the history books. The stadium was home to the Madrid Miners, a team which fed into the Brooklyn Dodgers and the Dodgers even played a game in the park to a packed house in 1934. The baseball park, still in operation is about to receive a substantial upgrading. It probably needed it after I'd spent a night there.

When the coal market collapsed, so did Madrid's infrastructure. Eventually the town's final residents moved away and Madrid became a ghost town. In 1954 the Wall Street Journal listed the entire town for sale for $250,000. By the 1960's and 70's an array of artists, crafts people and renegades rediscovered Madrid. Eventually the town's abandoned Victorian homes and clapboard storefronts were sold and new populations began to form in the town. Today's Madrid pioneers are local artists, craftspeople, gallery owners and business commuters to Santa Fe.

It had been a long day, but I felt satisfied with my distance. I wouldn't have expected to cover that mileage in the New Mexico heat in the mountains. Even better was that I found, when I checked online, that I was unlikely to be affected by the wildfires burning to the south. I could carry on in the morning. So I returned to the tent, had a quick check of the map by lamplight, and slept well.

Day 23 Wed 22 Jun
Madrid NM to Exit 140 on I-40
Distance 114 kms / 71 miles
Total so Far 2616 kms / 1634 miles
Accommodation: $100.00 Route 66 Casino Hotel

The alarm sounded at three in the morning and, despite my good intentions, I silenced it, in the hope of more sleep. It didn't happen so I got up at three-thirty, and packed up while waiting for water to boil. I was still full from the food of the night before and didn't feel the need to suffer oatmeal, so I satisfied myself with a chocolate drink before getting on the road.

Three hours of climbing uphill out of Madrid had me averaging eight miles an hour – or less. Still, once over the mountain, it was downhill to Albuquerque and breakfast at Cedar Crest, where the Verizon signal was good and strong. Like ET, I called home.

This city provided the usual urban challenge. The convoluted turns on the ACA maps always have the likelihood of me missing a turn, or going down a blind alley. I never found Dr Martin Luther King Jr Blvd, so I finally went past the University of New Mexico and braved the traffic on Central Ave to the Rio Grande and across the bridge out into the desert. It was a five-mile climb, which included a mile of roadworks – for which I was grateful. It gave me a break from the traffic as the lane on which I rode was off-limits to trucks. Love's Travel Stop, at the top, was a welcome pause and I crossed over the I-40 and had a soda and a water-bottle refill. I sat for half an hour to rebalance my temperatures. Outside, Marshall approached me, said he'd passed me by in his truck on the road and wondered if I was alright. He and his wife were feeling the heat in the air-conditioned cab of his eighteen-wheeler and he could only imagine what I was going through. He figured I just had to be in trouble. I said I was fine, but I wasn't going much farther. "Hats off to you, son," he said, and turned on his heel for the cool safety of his cab.

A mile along the frontage road, I came to an RV Park and considered stopping. They didn't allow tents so I'd no option but to carry on for the ten miles to the Casino Motel. I was now in the Navajo Nation and I had to stop because nothing was reachable after that. There was a Travel Centre – a stop for truckers – with a food court, but nowhere I'd have felt safe pitching a tent and I wasn't sure of the local by-laws. The safer option was to take a room – for me and the bike. One hundred dollars was more than I had been expecting to pay for accommodation and I had to tell myself that I could afford it.

Once my card was debited, I hauled Surly into an elevator and up to the fourth floor, to a room that was luxurious by the standards I'd come to know along the route. The two five-foot beds were a bit of overkill for a tired, solo cyclist, so I showered and rested before checking out the alien life forms in the casino. Rows and rows of slot machines beckoned and I must confess to having wagered some of my laundry quarters. A rattle and a ringing gave me a return of ten dollars and, ever the gambler, I put it on a dead cert – a chicken strips combo at the travel centre next door.

The next day's mileage would begin on the I-40, so no early start. I'd been feeling tired all day and hoped the air-conditioned room would revitalise me. I lay back on the big bed and surfed the news channels. There was still little news about the forthcoming presidential election. I was beginning to think it might be a damp squib. On the other hand, the UK electorate would be going to the polls to vote in a referendum on whether or not to leave the European Union. It didn't gain much traction on US television, probably because it was likely to be defeated. The alternative couldn't be countenanced.

Day 24 Thu 23 Jun
Exit 140 on I-40 to Grants NM
Distance 106 kms /66 miles
Total so Far 2722 kms / 1700 miles
Accommodation: $27.75 KOA Grants NM

I was, as usual, slow extricating myself from the room at six o'clock. At least I had the coffee-making facilities so I had myself a brew. The Dairy Queen supplied a hot dog and I bought myself a burrito to go. It would serve as my lunch, so I stowed it in the bar bag and pedalled off.

The journey to Grants was mostly flat or with little noticeable gradient but I had no option other than to ride the shoulder of I-40 for twenty-two miles to Mesita, where I rejoined the Old Route 66 into Laguna. In this Native American town, I went to the supermarket and I could see, even from the way the shelves were stocked that this area was in no way as prosperous as other similar-sized communities I'd come across.

Old Laguna was the first village of the pueblo. Its historic St. Joseph Mission Church, built in 1699, sits on the hill, visible for miles. The old village had a number of old adobe buildings in various states of repair. New Laguna had generally newer buildings and comprised mostly of homes. Three communities fairly close together was unusual and caused the miles to slip away. I stopped for a soda and stood in the air-conditioning of the warehouse-style general store. It obviously catered to all the needs of the community – and appeared to be the only store there. Paraje, three miles west of New Laguna, means "place" or "residence" and many villages were first called names like Paraje de Belen or Paraje de Bernalillo, because they served as a stopping point for travellers. The village is comprised mostly of homes and ruins of a few old buildings, but its active church continues to stand.

A Bud in Budville

I wasn't stopping here so I felt no need to explore the villages. I wasn't inundated with questions about my trip and didn't feel any great warmth. I stopped a few miles down the road. I mean, it would have been wrong not to have a Bud in Budville. Named for H.N. "Bud" Rice, it got its start when Bud and his wife Flossie opened an automobile service in 1928. Soon afterwards they opened the Budville Trading Company, and over the years -- a gas station, a few cabins, and the only tow company between the Rio Puerco River and Grants for a number of years. They also sold bus tickets, operated a post office, and Bud served as the Justice of Peace, a position in which he was known to have issued steep fines, especially to anyone outside of the area. Having operated the business for thirty-nine years, the store was held up by a desperado in November, 1967. There were four people in the building at the time -- Bud, Flossie, an 82-year old retired school teacher named Blanche Brown who worked part time, and a housekeeper named Nettie Buckley. Within moments, shots were fired and the gunman fled leaving behind a scene that would earn the trading post the nickname of "Bloodville." Fifty-Four year old Bud Rice and the elderly shop keeper Blanch Brown were dead. Flossie and the housekeeper survived. Though arrests were made, no one was ever convicted of the crime.

Flossie remarried a man named Max Atkinson and continued to run the family businesses. Six years after she had lost Bud, her second husband was killed in a fight in 1973, just feet from where Bud had been killed. Once again Flossie persevered and continued to run the business up until 1979, when its doors closed for good after sixty-six years in business. Somewhere along the line she married for a third time and passed away of natural causes in 1994.

I needed the break anyway. I had a quiet road, passed by only three cars in the space of an hour. It was typical desert countryside, with high outcrops, looking red against the black asphalt. At Paraje, I declined the Pueblo Alternative, shown on my map as a big climb to Sky City Cultural Center. Too much climbing – I'd done enough.

I travelled alongside the railroad and saw the produce of America being transported. Trains, one hundred carriages long, taking what seemed like ten minutes to pass, rumbled through with frequency, in both directions. All the engines carried the BNSF – Burlington Northern-Santa Fe – livery and the carriages were, a glossary of US manufacturing.

About five miles beyond McCarty's, Route 66 is crossed by the Great Divide Mountain Bike Route, which runs from Canada to the Mexican border. There, outside a Subway diner, was a parked mountain bike. I was almost finished for the day, so I pulled in hoping to have a fellow cyclist to chat with – even though we might speak a different biking language.

Fabrice was eating a sandwich inside. His bike carried minimal kit – in keeping with the philosophy of bikepacking. Fully loaded doesn't work off-road. I said hello and introduced myself. He was going north and wasn't even aware that Route 66 was passing this way. I wouldn't have been aware of the GDMBR if the map hadn't indicated it. I said I was going to Grants and would probably stay in a campsite. Fabrice wasn't sure. He'd been out of society since he started, sleeping where he could and hadn't considered paying a lot of money for accommodation. This brought me back to Laura and Noah in 2014, paying more for accommodation since they teamed up with the gang, whereas the same act had substantially lowered my costs.

We cycled together into Grants, where we parted. Fabrice was looking for a Walmart and I continued on as far as the campsite – it was just another KOA. I paid the fee and said that I might be joined by another – and that he should benefit from any reduction there might be for shared occupancy of the site. I was feeling generous.

Reading about Grants in the campsite office, I found that it had been a quiet farming community, but had taken advantage of the many travellers who came through town when Route 66 was built. Motels and services soon opened right up against the railroad tracks, many of which still operate today.

In 1950, a local rancher named Paddy Martinez found an odd yellow rock in the nearby Haystack Mountains ten miles west of town. The rock was uranium which created a booming economy in the area when the U.S. Atomic Energy Commission began to mine the valuable ore. It also started a fever among the locals as many invested in Geiger counters and took to the hills. Where never before had land been posted as "No Trespassing" it was now posted with "Trespassers Will be Prosecuted or Shot." Disputes between landowners regarding mineral rights claims became common and local attorneys had a field day.

The area's uranium reserves turned out to be one of the largest in the world and the population of Grants boomed from some twelve hundred people to nearly twelve thousand. The Grants uranium industry developed about six thousand jobs and produced about 63 percent of all the uranium mined in the United States. The mining continued in full force until the 1982-83 recession forced the closing of the mines and the mills.

The rain started, just as I got the tent up, complete with flysheet – a brief shower that cooled the day – and I made straight for the shower and laundry. Food followed – a tin of Campbell's chowder with Idahoan mashed potato. Everything was fine.

I relaxed, reading Steinbeck. The Joads had caught up with me and I was delighted with Steinbeck's description of the change in them after their days on the road. It was a description that only someone whose circumstances had altered radically could understand – "Thus they changed their social life – changed as in the whole universe only man can change. They were not farm men any more, but migrant men. And the thought, the planning, the long staring silence that had gone out to the fields, went now to the roads, to the distance, to the West. That man whose mind had been bound with acres lived with narrow concrete miles. And his thought and his worry were not any more with rainfall, with wind and dust, with the thrust of the crops. Eyes watched the tyres, ears listened to the clattering motors, and minds struggled with oil, with gasoline, with the thinning rubber between air and road" Their focused had changed dramatically. Their known world had been shattered and the pieces flung outwards to the point where they would never be recaptured. They had gone from the comfort of certainty, to the near-panic of uncertainty. My life on the road, compared with life at home, mirrored this experience but I had chosen to come on this trip. I had chosen to do it alone and I was, since my earlier trip, less prone to panic. I could make myself comfortable where I was. I could pay for comfort and I knew that, at the end of the day, no matter how hard the day on the bike was, I was on holiday.

That was what set me apart from those I'd seen in the earlier motels in Oklahoma. I was privileged and I should never forget it. Thanks, Steinbeck.

About quarter-to-seven, Fabrice appeared around the corner and shared my campsite. This resulted in a saving of five dollars for him. He was thankful, and presented me with the remains of his Pizza Hut pizza. I declined, explaining about my experience with the pizza in Tulsa and how that early morning taste of cold pizza lingered in my mind if not on my tongue.

Antiseptic spray brings a smile

Fabrice wondered where the campsite pool was and I explained that different campsites offered different facilities. This one included a breakfast in the price. I didn't think I'd be hanging around for a cup of coffee and a stale muffin in the morning, though. We chatted during the evening and my initial reticence in regard to the cold pizza was overcome. We nibbled at the remnants. Fabrice had a blister that had burst and was in danger of becoming a saddle sore. He was likely to take a rest day here. My hand had responded to the salt treatment and no longer bothered me, so I gifted him the antiseptic spray. It might help. This was a one-in-a-lifetime opportunity for him, a high-school teacher in France. He'd been bitten by the bikepacking bug and was taking on the daddy of them all. The last thing he needed was to have a saddle sore stop him in his tracks. He had until the end of August to complete the distance – over two thousand seven hundred miles.

Day 25 Fri 24 Jun
Grants NM to Zuni Pueblo NM
Distance 116 kms /72 miles
Total so Far 2838 kms / 1772 miles
Accommodation: Free: Catholic Mission in Zuni

Because small town American life ends about seven in the evening, I'd imagined that breakfast would have been from six-thirty and reconsidered waiting, and, anyway, going back into town to McDonalds was the alternative. I had to eat because there would be nothing for until I'd crossed the Continental Divide – about forty miles out. As it happened, breakfast, consisting of the expected cool coffee and muffin was from seven-thirty so I was an hour late getting on the road. I should have gone back to McDonalds, but, at least, I'd managed not to backtrack.

As I left Grants, I couldn't help but reflect on the USA and thoughts I might have had on the country previously. I don't know what it was that had influenced my thinking about the country – I suppose I was bombarded by liberal stories in Europe which coloured Uncle Sam as a war-mongering bully, spending phenomenal sums on the manufacture and export of armaments, of fomenting conflicts to achieve the end of supplying those armaments in pursuit of US economic interests. I mean, buying armaments isn't like buying a particularly hardwearing jacket where one will do. In the case of weapons, there's always the need for ammunition, and bombs, once dropped, must be replaced. Not only that, but once infrastructure is destroyed, it must be recreated.

But that, along with Silicon Valley and Hollywood, was only part of the story. Steinbeck had written of the removal of small farmers from the land, handing it over to banks and corporations. The farmers had to go somewhere. They went west. But what about the other land-based industries? Illinois had mined coal – the biggest lump of coal mined in the US had been taken out of the ground in Divernon IL. Zinc had been the mainstay of Joplin OK and Uranium had created Grants NM. These industries would have created employment and influenced large swathes of the land-based population living outside the primary centres of population. Just as the connecting of towns by Route 66 had brought prosperity and aspirations, the bypassing of those same towns by the interstate had rendered whole communities redundant. The closure of a railway line on a non-viable track might create the environment for a greenway, but the resentment of having a community's aspirations and hopes dashed by the railway's closure will be long-lasting. The only possible release for this resentment in a democracy will be at the ballot box. Where modernisation and development is to be welcomed, the economy must support society as much as society must support the economy. In some weird way, I felt that those who were advocating change away from the Democrats, would actually have more in common with the philosophy – and policies – of Bernie Sanders. But he was now gone. Who would they turn to? The election was being fought out on television. I'd seen very few daily newspapers – and I'd seen nobody reading them – in the diners and fast food outlets. Whoever spoke the language the voter could understand, whoever got to win the hearts of these passionate and God-fearing people would triumph. Logic had less to do with winning than appealing to the emotions. Luckily for the Democrats, only Donald Trump survived on the Republican side, so the outcome had to be pre-destined.

Sarky gets high

Any thoughts I might have had about a leisurely day disappeared with the uphill road from Grants and the temperatures rose hourly. I felt the distance to Gallup wasn't doable in one day and I'd intended only to go the forty-four miles to El Morro, where I would camp. It's always great to have a plan! I passed through El Malpais National Conservation Area and anyone with a smattering of either French or Spanish could figure that El Malpais meant "The Bad Country". If they couldn't figure it out, the ground would tell all. It was rough. The visitor centre didn't look inviting and certainly didn't look as if it would deliver fresh water so I continued climbing to the highest point on the trip. I was delighted to get over this almost seven thousand nine hundred-foot obstacle — sure, everything would now be downhill to the Pacific.

La Tinaja Restaurant — a roadside diner — was the first place on the route that I'd seen open on the downhill. I'd covered thirty-eight miles and I looked at my watch. Midday, so I ordered the burger and fries with a coke. A man there had seen me going up the hill and again on the downside. He asked me about the trip and where I was headed. When I said I was going to Gallup, he said that if I kept on this road, Hwy 53, to Zuni, there was a new link road which would take me to Sanders and save me, he said, sixty miles. Well, I'm not a purist and I was about to file this away. When I asked about accommodation along the way, the lady running the diner said there was an Irish priest, Fr Patrick — a lovely man — in St Anthony's Mission in Zuni. I should call by. I said I would if I went through, because a local perspective would be wonderful.

I briefly considered calling in to visit El Morro, basically a reliable waterhole in the New Mexico desert, but with my new schedule, I decided against it. Besides, I'd already seen the video online. I took a few pictures from the outside and passed on to Rameh, fighting the wind all the way. It had come out of nowhere — as if it was trying to stop me getting to Zuni. I remembered Ben's words "The reason there's wind in New Mexico is that Texas blows and Arizona sucks!" Finally, about half-five in the afternoon, I rolled up to an information office, where I asked about campsites. There were none. I asked about hotels and there was one. I asked about St Anthony's Mission and was given a map. Nothing more to be gained, I went down the street and turned right to the school.

A young lad appeared as I parked my bike against a fence, and asked if I was one of the bike group expected in tonight. No, I said, I was just passing through and dropped in to pay my respects to the Irish priest. He knew which door to go to and the priest answered. I introduced myself, explained how I came to be there and he said he was Scottish. I asked if there might be a patch of ground on which I could put a tent and the young lad said they were clearing out the cabins and maybe I might use one of those. Father Patrick Maguire said he'd see me later.

The young lad was part of a catholic mission from Maryland who'd spent time here in the Zuni Pueblo and were about to depart. They invited me to join them for food, but I was in no fit state to join anyone and needed my system to settle down so I just chatted for a while. Fr Maguire appeared and said he had a guest room I could use. It was teacher accommodation and, since they were on vacation, it was available. It had a bed, shower and coffee-making facilities. The latter swung it for me and Fr Pat unlocked the next door room for the bike. He said it was an attractive item. I felt as if I'd won the lotto. It turned out that the young lad I'd met was mistaken – the bike group would pass through a week later.

He returned after a previous engagement and said he was going to visit a Zuni family if I'd like to come along. I'd cleaned up after my dinner and was happy to join him. These parishioners were a very friendly family and insisted we eat with them. They were teachers in the school and were full of questions about Ireland, my trip and my background. My military background was very important to them because the father of the house, now deceased, had been a navy man. They'd considered that to be very honourable. I wondered to myself, why, when the Native American people had been treated so abysmally by successive administrations and by the white people, would they consider being able to serve in the armed forces of that power to be an honour. Perhaps they felt they were serving the country, not the government.

I was back in my room by nine and making plans for the next day. I'd eight litres of water distributed in various panniers for balance so the weight was considerable. Looking at the map, I saw that, in reality, I would only have saved twenty-five miles but, with nowhere to stay except El

Moro, and with big climbs shown on the map, I felt I'd done the right thing taking the Zuni option.

My hopes of either getting to know more about the Native American population or, indeed, Fr Maguire, were not realised. In reality, I would have needed to spend a lot more time in the area to become any wiser. People just don't open up to strangers, no matter how unthreatening they might appear on their bicycles. I wouldn't be around long enough to earn trust, though I couldn't fault their kindness. I found out from Zuni sources that Zuni Pueblo is the place of First Contact between Europeans and Native Peoples in the Southwest – an encounter that occurred over eighty years before the more widely known Plymouth Rock landing! Europeans first "discovered" Zuni territory in 1539 when Friar Marcos De Niza and a black Moorish former-slave named Estevanico led a party from Mexico in search of the fabled "Seven Cities of Cibola." The Spanish hoped that the stories they had heard about the "wealth" of this region meant "gold" or at least productive lands.

Francisco Vasquez de Coronado mounted a full expedition to explore and claim the fabled lands for Spain. A year later, in July 1540, his expeditionary force of about two thousand five hundred members, including almost four hundred Spaniards and the rest Amigos Indios – Mexican Indian allies, fought a battle that defeated the vastly outnumbered Hawikku warriors, who withdrew under cover of the night.

Their remoteness from Spanish settlements along the Rio Grande Valley, kept the Zunis isolated and they had only minimal contact with the Spanish during their years of colonisation in the region. New Mexico, including Zuni Pueblo, became United States Territory in 1848 and continued appropriation and abuse of Zuni lands by the government and unscrupulous land grabbers led to the shrinkage of Zuni's aboriginal territories and their confinement to a reservation a small fraction of the original size of Zuni's original land-use areas.

Not understanding the issues didn't prevent me drawing superficial conclusions about the pueblo. The main road through the settlement was paved, while most other streets were dirt roads. Homes seemed to be mostly pre-fabricated dwellings set on individual dirt sites. This wasn't surprising as the town was set in, what appeared to me to be a desert. There was little evidence of industry or agriculture. Tourism didn't seem to feature greatly. All in all, the environment reminded me of townships I'd come across in Kenya or Angola in the nineties. But, I countered in my own mind, some of the trailer parks I'd seen along Route 66 had been quite pitiful too and I'd wondered how the residents survived. At least, gambling was legal in the Indian lands – I'd spent a night at the Route 66 Casino – and that is a valuable source of income. My last thought was for the work being done by Fr Maguire and his parishioners. It was a long way for him from his home in Dunblane, Scotland – famous as the birthplace of tennis player, Andy Murray, and the scene of a school massacre, which killed sixteen people twenty years ago.

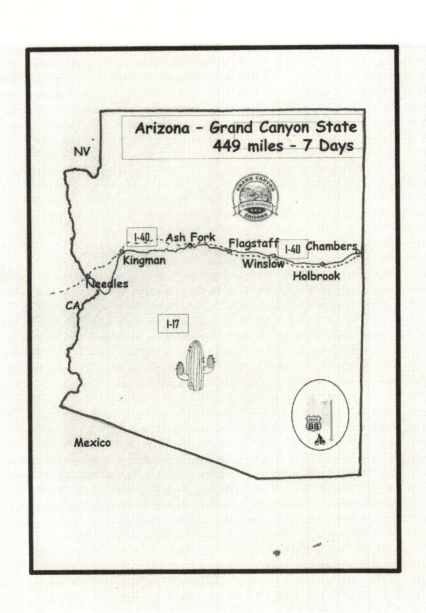

Chapter 7

Arizona – Grand Canyon State

Day 26 Sat 25 Jun
Zuni Pueblo NM to Chambers AZ
Distance 77 kms /48 miles
Total so Far 2915 kms / 1820 miles
Accommodation: $70.00 Days Inn, Chambers AZ

The fortuitous burger stop in the La Tinaja restaurant had secured me free accommodation, a shortcut and good company for an evening. I couldn't have asked for more from a day on the road. The compound, in which I was the only occupant, had a picnic table, which provided a suitable platform for me to ready myself for travelling. The clean water replenished all receptacles and I had oatmeal and chocolate drink to start the day, shortly after dawn.

The early morning air was still and I had the road to myself as I pedalled along, fresh after a good night's sleep. Twelve miles from Zuni, Hwy 53 became Hwy 61 and New Mexico became Arizona. Nothing else changed – the desert was still desert, the silence was as profound and the landscape was totally devoid of wildlife. It was wildly beautiful here in the high desert and I would enjoy the next four hundred miles of the Grand Canyon state at its most picturesque. There would be volcanoes, painted deserts and lush green forests – according to the blurb. Most importantly right now, I would be opening up a new set of maps once this day ended. It seemed a very short time since I'd opened this set in Adrian TX. I was twenty-six days out from Chicago and only two states separated me from the ocean. I'd long ago accepted that this was really going to be a solo trip. I'd given up on the idea that I might have some company on the road. From here, I'd be lucky if I even saw a car for the next while.

Turning off Hwy 61 onto Northwell Road, the shortcut mentioned to me in the Tinaja restaurant, I really owned the world. Evidence of previous wildfires was everywhere. Charred trunks of stunted trees proliferated, but, in its resilience, the desert was showing evidence of new scrub. I had five miles of gentle descent on a good new surface, black against the bleached badlands, to join Hwy 191, and sixteen miles to Sanders along a good shoulder where I had my real breakfast at the Mustang gas station. Coffee and a burrito set me up for the last few miles to Chambers along the frontage road beside the I-40. I'd decided to go only as far as Chambers because the map indicated limited services west of Gallup for almost one hundred and twenty miles. There would be seventy empty miles the next day, so I'd better rest up today.

There were no rooms ready in the Days Inn in Chambers AZ, when I got there. I'd just have to wait, so I sat in the lobby, where it was cool. Between nodding off and munching the complimentary candies in the bowl on the table, the time passed and I finally got a room. That my credit card was declined and I had to use cash, was a concern to me.

The number in Bank of Ireland wasn't manned by the time I got through on Skype, so that would be a job for the morning before getting on the road again. I could have used my Visa Debit card but I didn't want to expose that card at all. It would only be used as an absolutely last resort.

It was a long day to put in after a short cycle. Other than the motel – and a gas station where I went to eat – there was nothing in the area. I showered, rested and read. Surfing the news channel, I saw that Britain had voted to leave the European Union. What next? Trump for president? The latter might not be so fanciful. All along my route, I'd only met those who intensely disliked – or hated – Hillary Clinton and were going to vote for whoever the Republican Party chose. Some might have even considered Bernie Sanders – though they thought him a communist – but he was now out of the contest.

I used the hotel WiFi to browse the internet and find information about what I might expect in Arizona – it all seemed to promise an exciting time as I crossed the state. Initially, I'd be on the I-40 shoulder until I reached the Painted Desert and Petrified Forest. All my stuff was ready for an early departure the next morning, because I'd unpacked little. The hotel room carried a complimentary breakfast from six-thirty, so I'd avail of that. There were so many channels on television but, with so little choice or content, I turned off the light at nine-fifteen.

Day 27 Sun 26 Jun
Chambers AZ to Holbrook AZ
Distance 118 kms /74 miles
Total so Far 3033 kms / 1894 miles
Accommodation: $27.85 KOA Holbrook

The I-40, my route for the first twenty-two miles, allowed me to reflect on this morning so far. I'd called the bank in Ireland and they'd said they hadn't declined my card – that it must have been a glitch with the card reader in the hotel. They said they were aware of my trip and that they were tracking my progress across the US. I felt like I had my own financial fan club! The girl was very friendly. I'd called them before leaving to give them my route so I wouldn't have an experience as I had in 2014, when a purchase was queried by the bank in a text. So my card was still fine and I was relieved. Breakfast in the hotel would taste all the better.

The restaurant attached to the hotel was closed – even the clock in the lobby was wrong, showing five-fifteen. I couldn't raise anyone by knocking on the counter and finally I saw a note telling me to use the phone for assistance. The duty manager appeared and I retrieved the deposit I'd paid the previous day. He looked tired and dishevelled and, when I complained about the restaurant being closed, he explained an hour change I hadn't been aware of. I'd made a major mistake by not passing through Gallup – I'd have been alerted to a one-hour time difference on entering Arizona. That explained the wait for the room to be readied at the hotel. Now I was on Californian time and the last change before the end. It also explained why I'd have to wait another hour for a cup of coffee.

Luckily, the gas station next door was open. On my way in, I was approached by a man who said he was hitching from Flagstaff to Albuquerque and had been abandoned by a truck-driver in Chambers. He'd no money and asked if I'd spare the price of a cup of coffee. He hadn't eaten since the previous day. I told him to get a coffee and to pick up a sandwich from the limited range available and I paid the attendant. Outside, he thanked me and asked if I might spare the price of a packet of cigarettes? "Ah, here!" I thought to myself. But I remembered how much I had enjoyed a cigarette, back in the day when I smoked, and how smoking worked as an appetite suppressant. He might need all the help he could get, so I contributed to his addiction and left – before he caught me for the price of a bottle of whiskey!

I was well ahead of time when I reached the entrance to the Petrified Forest National Park and met a group of Japanese taking photographs. The one who could speak English asked me about the trip and translated for the others. Then he asked me how old I was and he said – with the great authority longevity had conferred on him – that sixty was very young. There was a lot of smiling and half-bowing as they took my picture and then used my phone to take one for me. The park was open, but the diner inside the gate didn't open until eight. I wasn't going to wait half an hour so I picked up a few bits for an exorbitant price in the gift shop next door.

I had thirty wonderful miles of cycling through the park, once I'd paid the ten dollars entrance fee. Every few hundred yards demanded a stop to take pictures. The Painted Desert lived up to its name with colourful views out to fifty miles in the clear air from rocky overlooks. I was ahead of the main crowd, I thought, because the traffic was light. I played leapfrog with the Japanese group as they also stopped along the route. I was very taken with the Petrified Forest – fossilised remains of trees – some pieces were ten metres long. Steinbeck had the Joads looking out on the Painted Desert when they arrived, only to be told by a border guard to keep going. The old 1932 Studebaker on the side of the road evoked memories of when Route 66 cut through the Park. There was even a small stretch of the original paved route. It would have been much more exciting if I hadn't seen similar in Missouri, Kansas, Oklahoma and Texas. I was following the Joad family's journey, but I had to realise that Route also opened up the West for tourists from the east and Middle America who wanted to visit the Grand Canyon and California. A trip from Middle America to the coast could take about a week. For many, the journey was not just across miles, it was across culture and lifestyles, from the modest to the exotic. Of course, getting to your destination was important, but the trip itself across more than two thousand miles was a reward. From the neon signs of one-of-a-kind motels to burgers and chicken fried steaks in the multitude of restaurants; from the filling stations that served as miniature oases to gaudy tourist traps, citizens got to experience the post-war magic of internal travel on the open road.

It was a gradual downhill from the high desert to the almost-dry Little Colorado River at Holbrook. I admired the fantastic pieces at the entrance to Jim Gray's Petrified Wood sales depot and thought how cool they would look in a garden in Ireland. I hadn't totally gone bush! I turned onto Apache Ave and Navajo Blvd to the Dairy Queen for lunch.

Holbrook was initially a cowboy and cattle town and welcomed the money of the cattle company and its associated cowboys, until they saw the downside. The buckaroos of the outfits quickly gained the unsavoury reputation of being the "thievinist, fightinest bunch of cowboys" in the United States. Many of the cowboys working for the Hashknife Outfit were wanted men and on two occasions, were linked to train robberies locally at Canyon Diablo. The sudden presence of so many cowboys also gave rise to rustling, robbery and gunfights. Much of the rustling was done against the Hashknife Outfit itself. Stagecoach robberies became an almost recreational pastime for cowboys and drifters in the area. And, when the cowboys came off the range, with money in their pockets and whiskey on their minds, it was time for Holbrook to "look-out!" In 1886 alone, there were twenty-six shooting deaths on the streets of Holbrook, which was called home to only about 250 people at the time.

Sheriff Commodore Perry Owens is credited with bringing law and order to the wild and crusty town in 1887. It all started when a warrant against a man named Andy Cooper was issued for cattle rustling. In actuality, Cooper was one Andy Blevins, who had changed his name when he came to Arizona because of an outstanding warrant for murder in Texas.

When Owens went to the Blevins family home on September 4, 1887, the family was in the midst of Sunday dinner and Cooper, aka Blevins, refused to come out. Within moments, Andy's half brother, John, opened the door and took a shot at the sheriff, who quickly drew both of his six-guns, sending bullets into both John and Andy. A gunfight inevitably ensued and Sam Blevins, just 15 years-old, ran out the door firing at Owen, who returned the shots. A friend of the Blevin family named Mose Roberts also fired upon the Sheriff. The melee lasted less than a minute and Andy and Sam Blevin, as well as Mose Roberts, were killed. John Blevins was wounded. Today, the historic site of the gunfight still stands on Central Avenue in Holbrook.

By the time Route 66 made its appearance, the wild and lawless town had become more settled, and the narrow strip of asphalt became a symbol of hope to the city and the many travellers of the Mother Road, when the gas shortage was over after World War II ended. Dozens of souvenir shops opened, offering samples of petrified wood and Indian Treasures. In 1950, the Wigwam Village, which continues to serve customers, was built.

Holbrook might have tempted me and I'd have loved a beer, but the one bar, where I stopped, was closed until the evening. The KOA campsite, three miles uphill from the pub, didn't encourage a return to town later on. The darkening sky worried me and, expecting the worst, I pitched the tent firmly. I piled everything inside and took shelter as the wind came up. There was no rain, but the tents took a battering that caused two families to upgrade to a cabin. I sat it out in a pavilion, the slatted sides of which served as a bit of a wind break. The bonus of a swimming pool in this KOA was wasted as nobody was going to venture into those choppy waters.

By six-thirty, the wind had died down enough to reassure me that I might not have to spend a night sheltering in the washroom. I ate a dehydrated meal before settling down for the night as I considered the day to have been a good one. I'd broken through the three-thousand kilometre barrier.

Day 28 Mon 27 Jun
Holbrook AZ to Meteor Crater AZ
Distance 100 kms /62 miles
Total so Far 3133 kms / 1956 miles
Accommodation: $28.75 Meteor Crater RV Park

The hour change had me screwed up. I was up and about at four. I thought I was supposed to make a call at six, but it turned out that it was at five. Packing was more time-consuming because I'd stripped everything from the bike to anchor the tent in the wind. The "all you can eat" breakfast of coffee and pancakes wasn't available until seven. I wouldn't wait for it and headed to McDonalds for breakfast. This McDonalds seemed to have hidden all the power outlets and getting to one while being able to keep an eye on the bike was tricky. I must have looked odd, mooching around before ordering. The breakfast sandwich and coffee was fine and I topped up the phone charge while I finished off the refill. I filled the water bottles with iced water and got going.

I knew the early morning coolness wouldn't last though I was still at about five thousand feet in elevation. It was easy to forget the altitude, but maybe I'd feel the difference in my breathing when I got back to sea level. By my reckoning, I had only about five hundred miles to cover to get to the coast, but it was full of challenges. I was in the "wild west" now and the landscape wasn't the lush forestry of the Ozarks. Sharp, rocky and unforgiving, it required a certain type of person with particular strengths to survive and live in this land which was picturesque to the visitor – just as the small fields on the Aran Islands are so pretty when viewed by the tourist from the capital. Collecting hand-won turf from the bog seems like a romantic thing to do, when one doesn't have to do it. Staying in RV Parks was all part of my adventure – but how much of an adventure was it for those who had no other choice. I would have to understand that those who lived out in this land here operated as frontiersmen battling extreme elements rather than living with the conveniences of large communities. Their priorities are different – WiFi might be slightly less important than drinking water – and once I was aware of this, I might, finally, get to understand the sub-culture a little more.

I stayed on the downhill shoulder of I-40 rather than the Route 66 to Joseph City, saving me three miles. They all count! The frontage road from there to Jackrabbit road must have been part of the original Route 66. The surface was dreadful and I was almost happy to get back on the I-40 to Winslow. I hadn't been familiar with the lyrics of the Eagles classic, Take it Easy and I had wondered when people had told me to be sure and take a picture on the corner of Winslow.

Well, I'm a-standin' on a corner in Winslow, Arizona
Such a fine sight to see
It's a girl, my Lord, in a flat-bed Ford
Slowin' down to take a look at me
Come on, baby, don't say maybe
I gotta know if your sweet love is gonna save me
We may lose and we may win, though we will never be here again
So open up I'm climbin' in, so take it easy

– Glenn Frey & Jackson Browne

Standin' on the Corner

When the town was bypassed by I-40 in the 1970s, tourism died and businesses began to close their doors. In a twist of fate, The Jackson Browne and Glenn Frey song "Take it Easy", which became an Eagles classic in 1972, just happened to mention Winslow Arizona and put the town on the national map of consciousness. This had been pure coincidence as neither songwriter had ever been to the town before the song was written – it just fitted the metre of the lyrics!

The downtown of Winslow was frozen in time once the town was bypassed. The railroad announced plans to move out of Winslow for good in 1994, and the famous Harvey Hotel, La Posada, was scheduled for demolition. Realising the threat to the town, and the tourist possibilities, the townspeople took action. First on the list of items to save was the old hotel, which they did. Second was the restoration of Winslow's downtown historic district, which continues to this day. I found the corner, a manufactured park inspired by the Eagles' song, on Kinsley Ave, and had my picture taken beside the statue erected to represent the song. Queues of tourists waited their turn – and it was only ten-thirty!

Though it was too early for lunch, the coffee shop opposite the park looked inviting. I ordered oatmeal with fruit and nuts with a double espresso. Maybe I was being finicky, but I was really looking forward to a bit of class for my – almost – ten dollars. The espresso arrived in a paper cup, like a small McDonalds cup, sugar was at the end of the counter and there were plastic stirrers. I'd finished the coffee by the time my oatmeal arrived and I complained that I'd asked for them to be brought – at the same time. They eventually brought me another one – obviously tolerant of a curmudgeonly old man!. The oatmeal was lovely, but what's this preoccupation with plastic cutlery? I'd have been reluctant to leave a tip, if I hadn't had to pay in advance for the service. It was the only café on THAT corner in Winslow AZ, so whether or not I'd recommend it would probably make no difference.

It was uphill for twenty-two miles into a stiff headwind on the shoulder of the I-40 to the rest area where I stopped for a break only to find the rear wheel was soft. It was the new tyre – the one I'd purchased in Amarillo

TX – so I hoped it was only a slow puncture. There was no drinking water available and no cold drinks for sale either. I just rested for a while. My campsite for the night wasn't far down the road and I pumped the tyre and carried on. There was a bang and the wheel was flat again. Now I was worried. At least I hadn't yet left the rest area so I had access to a table where I could unload the bike and organise myself in the heat.

The tyre I'd bought in Amarillo had let me down with less than a thousand kilometres done. The internal casing had shredded and couldn't support the tube. I pumped again and it held, after a fashion, for the three miles to the Meteor Crater RV Park. There would be no more miles put down today.

The site for the tent, at $28.75, was pricey – but they always are for the solo traveller. I got the tent up and set about organising myself against the ever-darkening sky. There might be a storm. The wheel was next. I swopped the tyre from the front to the back wheel to take the weight off the rear one. The new tyre was useless, so that just left the old damaged one. I cut three layers of tubing to act as a boot inside the tyre – when I discovered that it was a puncture repair kit I'd been given in the bike shop in Santa Fe – and inserted a new tube. I put it on the front wheel and pumped it. I'd check it in the morning to see if it was going to bring me the forty miles to Flagstaff. There were a number of bike shops there and no doubt I'd get sorted there.

I lingered under the hot shower to wash away my irritation with the wheel. I had time on my hands, because it was too windy to set up the stove for my dinner. I didn't want to tempt fate with the bike, so I skipped the trip down to the actual Meteor Crater which was formed approximately fifty thousand years ago when an iron mass, weighing over sixty thousand tons entered the Earth's atmosphere, resulting in the formation which is about four thousand feet wide and five hundred and seventy feet deep. The most important statistic was that it was six miles from the campsite – too far for me.

The clouds failed to deliver on the promise of higher winds or rain, so I could relax. All in all, I'd had a good day. The temperature in the morning had made cycling pleasurable and I'd gotten off the road before I ran into serious problems. Tomorrow would bring me to the "cool" town of Flagstaff.

Day 29 Tue 28 Jun
Meteor Crater AZ to Flagstaff AZ
Distance 67 kms /42 miles
Total so Far 3200 kms / 2000 miles
Accommodation: $28.75 Du Beau Hostel

It was with a sense of trepidation that I got out of the sleeping bag in the dark at four-thirty. Would the tyre be hard? Would it last the ride? If I broke down, would there be help available? I'd never had these doubts before and it is a measure of the fragility of my existence on the road – the absence of alternatives – that these thoughts became anxieties, if not worries. I'd heard it said that the Irish are optimistic, never worrying about Plan B – but that was because they couldn't afford a Plan B. Still, I'd done what I could – the bad tyre – my weakest link – was on the front wheel with least weight pressing down on it. I hoped for luck and a tailwind! I waited until I'd finished my breakfast before testing the wheel. I didn't want to face failure on an empty stomach – and, anyway a pleasure delayed and all that. The tyre had held overnight so I was worry-free again!

I was on the road at six-twenty. The temperatures were good and I made good time to Winona where I stopped for coffee and a bun. I parked my bike outside the front window of Mary's Cafe where I could keep an eye on it and took a booth inside. The guy in the next booth said I didn't need to worry about somebody stealing my bike because the local bike thief had gotten killed the week before. It seems he stole a bike across the street, but got hit by a car fifty feet from where he stole the bike. "Talk about bad karma," said the waitress as she walked by. I had only fifteen miles to climb from here to arrive Flagstaff, at seven thousand feet, and it felt like I hadn't cycled at all.

There are versions of how Flagstaff got its name and all centre around the stripping of a lone pine tree and making it into a flagpole. It had several names – Antelope Spring, Flagstaff, and Old Town – before settling. The Atlantic and Pacific Railroad (now the Santa Fe) came through in 1882 and the ten buildings in Old Town moved closer to the new railroad depot. A post office was established and assumed the name of Flagstaff. With the new railroad, the lumber and cattle businesses began to thrive, assuring the growth of the community.

Three brothers, Michael, Tim, and Denis Riordan were some of the first to profit from the lumber when they formed the Arizona Lumber and Timber Company. My whole trip had thrown up Irish connections to opening up the Territories and the West. Though Denis would soon move on to California, Michael and Tim would remain in the community making essential contributions to its development, including bringing electricity to Flagstaff and building nearby Lake Mary.

The University of Northern Arizona was established in 1899 and Flagstaff became the cultural centre of Northern Arizona. By the early 1900s, Flagstaff's wonders had become well known and tourism became its biggest industry. Flagstaff continued to grow at a slow and steady pace.

Route 66 created business for Flagstaff and the Historic Downtown, today, still sports a number of vintage cafes and motor courts. I was looking forward to getting there. Accommodation in town shouldn't be a problem – a university town during vacation should, despite the tourism boom, provide a weary cyclist with a cheap room.

Flagstaff stands as the gateway to many nearby national parks and monuments – Sunset Crater National Monument, Walnut Canyon National Monument, Wupatki National Monument, and Grand Canyon National Park, as well as Petrified Forest National Park, through which I'd pedalled a couple of days previously. These sights seemed close – and would be to a motorist – but to a cyclist they were out of reach, unless I took time off the bike and rented a car.

Legend has it that somewhere on a mountain ledge overhanging the City of Flagstaff, Arizona is buried an approximate $125,000 taken from a stage coach in 1881. East of Flagstaff at Canyon Diablo, the Atlantic and Pacific Railroad was the end of the line for those heading to California. As the stage coach passengers waited, four canvas mail bags were unloaded from the train to the westbound coach. Onlookers watched as the mail bags were transferred from the train to the boot of the coach, noticing that two of the bags appeared to be particularly heavy.

With the baggage loaded, the coach headed west onto the California-Santa Fe Trail and Flagstaff. The passengers and baggage would meet the next stage en route to another railroad at Needles, California. The gradient was extreme and the team of horses climbed steadily along the San Francisco Peaks until they reached a flat divide. It hadn't changed much for cyclists either.

Five riders surrounded the coach levelling their six-guns at the passengers and the crew. The bandit leader immediately motioned two of the outlaws to the back of the coach, where the two lifted out the two heavy mail sacks, dropping them to the ground and the coach – and its unmolested passengers – was sent on its way and reached Flagstaff – a collection of wooden shacks, two stores and five saloons, one of which served as the local stage station.

The terrified passengers disembarked, talking excitedly about the stage hold-up. Nearby, the station agent listened to the account and pulled the stage master aside. Still confused as to why any outlaws would be interested in nothing but mailbags, the stage master learned that the two bags taken contained a shipment of gold and silver bound from an Albuquerque Bank to a San Francisco Bank. The Station Manager explained that Wells Fargo, who had been plagued by a rash of recent stage coach robberies, had attempted to fool any future bandits by packing the gold and silver into two-five gallon whiskey kegs in each bag. It must have been an inside job.

Wells-Fargo, no doubt embarrassed by their ill-conceived idea, demanded the help of the U.S. Army. A patrol of the 6th US Cavalry picked up the bandit trail with the help of two Indian scouts. The twelve-man cavalry followed the robbers to an elevation of 8,500 feet to a log cabin where five saddled horses were tethered to a pole corral. The bandits were prepared to mount and ride off when the troopers rushed them. The outlaws opened fire and it was returned. All five outlaws lay dead. The bandits' horses and equipment were gathered up and the cabin was searched, but no loot was found. Word, of course quickly spread, and the very next day more than a dozen men arrived in the area searching for the hidden loot. The entire area was searched and dug up, but still nothing was found. Within a few months the robbery was all but forgotten to most.

The property owner, George Veit, diligently searched for the stolen treasure for almost thirty years – digging all over the slopes, the dirt floor of the cabin, around the spring and in the nearby perpetual ice caves. But he never found the cache. Family members and other treasure hunters followed but to date no one has ever claimed to have found the treasure. Maybe I should consider taking time off.

The smell from the Purina Dog Food Facility on the outskirts made me think it should be twinned with Kildare town in Ireland. I'd been well-acquainted with that smell from the chilling factory in the eighties and nineties – and, anyway, the Curragh of Kildare has its own Flagstaff south of the Curragh Camp. It had been a major reference point for us cadets during our training at the Military College in the late seventies and Mel Gibson filmed scenes for Braveheart on its slopes.

I had visions, before I saw it, of Flagstaff being similar in architecture to Santa Fe – a frontier town proud of its heritage. I mean, it was so far from civilisation that it couldn't be anything else, surely? My first view of this city of sixty-five thousand people reminded me of an encounter I had in Bosnia in 1997. I was an election monitor – one of many from all over the world. It was my first meeting with people from the "Stans" – Kazakhstan, Uzbekistan, Tajikistan, and Kyrgyzstan. I was very interested when Daniel said he was from Almaty. Knowing that it was in the centre of Asia – and knowing nothing else – I asked what they built their homes from. "Same as here," he'd replied, and I felt a little sheepish. Did I think they lived in mud huts or yurts? I had the same sense of having prejudged wrongly here in Flagstaff, but I didn't have time to dwell on it as the black clouds which had kept me company from dawn, delivered rain that was only going to get heavier.

I shared the shelter of the Burger King doorway with another vagrant. We chatted while the rain bounced off the pavement. I could be here for a while. Looking around, I saw a laundrette and had an idea. I asked Tim if he'd fancy a coffee and breakfast sandwich. "Sure would," he replied, so I asked him to mind the bike and I'd be back in a couple of minutes. Taking my swimming trunks and a t-shirt from my pack, I changed out of my cycling clothes in the Burger King washroom, then bought the breakfast and brought it out to Tim. He thanked me and I wheeled the bike across the forecourt to the laundrette.

Sitting in just my swimming trunks – everything else was in the wash – I could watch the bike. I must have looked like the male model in a Levis ad

– who'd aged particularly badly. Still, it got my clothes clean and I got shelter until the rain stopped.

I got a message from Patty, from Blanding UT. She and Bruce had been planning to come down to Flagstaff to meet me but they'd been caught up with farming matters in Cortez. I'd already thought that driving four hundred miles, just to say hello to the Irishman who'd stayed with them for a night in 2014, seemed a bit crazy, but hey, I'm not American. The difference between Ireland and America is that, in Ireland, one hundred miles is a long way, while, in America, one hundred years is a long time!

Refreshed – and in clean apparel – I got back on the bike to pedal the few remaining miles to find accommodation in the centre of town. When I came to Absolute Bikes on the way, I decided to give them my sob story. Some bike shops, especially those that look classy, might not be open to abandoning their schedule to assist a walk-in. I was hoping that me being a long-distance traveller would appeal to their better nature. I wasn't disappointed. They couldn't have been nicer. Tom swopped out the damaged tyre and complimented me on getting to Flagstaff on my workaround repair. He offered a Specialized Roubaix Pro as the best replacement they had. I went with that and, when I saw it was a foldable tyre, I got a second – just so I'd have a spare. He fitted the replacement and binned the damaged one. He cleaned the gear mechanism and the brakes, oiled the chain and tightened varying nuts and bolts and refused to take money other than for the tyres themselves.

Now, with laundry and bike sorted, my mental checklist was being ticked off – find accommodation, shower, change clothes, find a micro-brewery and sample the local brew. I didn't have long to wait. Right in the centre of the Historic Downtown, on Route 66, I found Du Beau Hostel, just behind the train station. A private room was sixty-nine dollars. I thought it steep, but the tourist season was up and running and they had no shared dorm beds left. I was lucky to get their last room. It included breakfast in the morning. The brew-pub across the street sealed the deal!

With the bike unpacked and stowed in the room, I got myself cleaned up and lay back on the bed to relax. I'd made good time and was finished early. I wouldn't take a rest day because there was nobody to share the time with – and, anyway, this had been a day short enough to be almost considered a rest day. Had Patty and Bruce driven down, I might have taken a day or two. I was only eighty miles south of the Grand Canyon and it would have made an interesting side trip. There were many other reasons for staying – not least the boast of the guy on reception, who declared that this college town of sixty-five thousand had thirty-five bars. I didn't want to boast about Galway, where you could visit the top ten pubs and not have scratched the surface – or left the main street!. Still, when most communities didn't have a single pub, this number was really significant.

My Road companion

Imagine a pub nowadays without WiFi. Well, I found it at my first attempt. Brews and Cues opposite the hostel had a good beer and I sat by the window, more for light to read by than to watch the world go by. Steinbeck's Joad family had outstripped me. "They crawled up the slopes and the low twisted trees covered the slopes. Holbrook, Joseph City, Winslow. And then the tall trees began, and the cars spouted steam and labored up the slopes. And there was Flagstaff, and that was the top of it all. Down from Flagstaff over the great plateaus, and the road disappeared in the distance ahead. The water grew scarce, water has to be bought, five cents, ten cents, fifteen cents a gallon. The sun drained the rocky country, and ahead were the jagged broken peaks, the western wall of Arizona. And now they were in flight from the sun and the drought. They drove all night, and came to the mountains in the night. And they crawled the jagged ramparts in the night, and their dim lights flickered on the pale walls of the road." In the space of a paragraph, he managed to give them a lead of almost two hundred miles and four days on me and he injected a sense of fear into me, their pursuer. This trip was about to get serious, if his descriptions were accurate. They had been, so far, so I'd no reason to doubt them. Nothing for it but to order another beer!

I finished up and wandered on, taking in the murals and the atmosphere. The Lumberyard Brewing Company was ticking over nicely — a nice vibrant crowd sitting in the open air eating and drinking. I settled at a table and ordered beer and wings, so I could take in the surroundings and earwig on conversations around me. I was drawn to the chat from the next table where a British accent spoke about Brexit. I took my time, but finally introduced myself as an Irishman and asked if I might join their table. Malcolm and Bob were both on the staff of the Northern Arizona University and their attitude and conversation was a dramatic change from the conservative views I'd had since Chicago. I wondered if the world was changing for me. I'd been starved of conversation and was delighted with this lively exchange. We sat together for an hour before they had to leave. Bob was from Flagstaff while Malcolm had arrived here twenty years previously. I remarked that the town seemed an expensive place to visit or live in and they said it had "millionaire views on a vagrant's budget". It was a wonderful society with its views moderated by the student population. Its accessibility by train from the West Coast was another civilising factor, they said. But they had a warning for me "Don't even THINK of having a conversation like this in Kingman – it's a completely different society! A college town, it ain't."

With Malcolm and Bob in Flagstaff

They left and I finished up, heading along through town to explore on my own until it began to get dark. Then it was back to the hostel at the end of a very satisfying day. It's all about the company!

Day 30 Wed 29 Jun
Flagstaff AZ to Ash Fork AZ
Distance 85 kms /53 miles
Total so Far 3285 kms / 2053 miles
Accommodation: $29.00 Ash Fork Inn

Breakfast was from seven and I'd normally have had two hours cycling under my belt by then. I needed to understand that there was life beyond the bike and, at nearly eight o'clock, I seated myself, with a coffee and Danish, at a table in the courtyard of the hostel in the soft morning sunshine. I dawdled, determined to get the benefit of the room price. I had planned a shortish day and, with a height gain of only about one thousand feet and a drop of over three thousand, this seemed like it would be a pleasant day out. I had Steinbeck and my journal for company so I wouldn't appear to be a lonely old git.

A woman emerged from the room beside mine and joined me, introducing herself as Lisa. She was travelling with her son, she said, who normally lived with her ex-husband in Tuscany, Italy. She felt he needed to see the States. I was thinking of a young spoilt Italian ponce, until he appeared – a strapping young man in a Leinster Rugby shirt. Confident and with perfect English, he hoped to have a career in rugby. He'd attended a number of Leinster summer camps and once I proclaimed myself a Munster supporter, we had a great chat. Lisa was somewhat awed by my trip so far, more so because I was travelling alone. "Must get lonely?" Being alone kept me moving, I said, and travelling solo means never having to say "sorry". Otherwise it would be too easy to stop for a few days to explore. "On the other hand" I said, "if I was sitting at the table with another person, would you have felt as comfortable about sitting down?" She agreed that it would have been more challenging, but I said that I would love to have a like-minded travelling companion – and then I pointed to Steinbeck. Lisa had read it and said it was a real tragedy, but with an element of redemption. I hadn't found any of the latter yet, but I'd only lost sight of them as they drove past Flagstaff. "Don't worry," she laughed, "you'll catch up with them in Needles, but you mightn't like what you find!"

They'd come to Flagstaff on the Amtrak Southwest Chief from Chicago. It had been an amazing journey across Illinois, Missouri, Kansas and Colorado, before swinging south to get around the Rockies. They'd stay three days here and had hired a car to go to the Grand Canyon. I envied them their comfort and the time off, but I knew that once I got back on the road, I'd be fine. It's not good to mix with settled people for too long.

The I-40 was my only way west out of Flagstaff and it ran beside the railroad so the first miles were punctuated by train hooters and noisy rolling stock. For the first time, I saw an interstate sign indicating Los Angeles and convinced myself that I was nearly there, though I knew that the hardest part of the journey was really still ahead. I'd broken the two thousand mile barrier the previous day and hadn't even been aware of it until writing up my journal.

Light at the end of the tunnel?

About twenty miles out, I drifted away from the interstate and railroad and crossed the Arizona Divide at seven thousand three hundred feet to pass through Parks, a little settlement with one store, doubling as a post office. It originally began as nothing more than a depot in an old boxcar in 1898 and hadn't progressed much since then.

A highway was built from Parks to the Grand Canyon in 1921 and another store – with a gas station – opened at the intersection of what would later become Route 66 and Spring Valley Road. This old store, the Pines General Store, predates the Mother Road and continues to serve travellers today. I had a coffee and a bun there and took a break in the woodland setting. It was just magical to sit under trees and smell the pines after days in the desert. It was a pity I'd discovered this piece of heaven so early in the morning – when heat and tiredness hadn't yet hit me. I would certainly fantasise about camping spots like this!

Over the next ten miles I had one sharp hill to climb before I dropped into Williams which, like the rest of the West, had been home to many Native American Tribes for thousands of years. Later Spanish explorers would first see the Grand Canyon while searching for the Seven Cities of Cibola in the mid 1500s. They must have been amazed when they came across that massive canyon, after having travelled hundreds of miles over nothing but desert sand.

In the early nineteenth century, mountain men began to push west in search of the plentiful game, when the fur trade was at an all time high. One of these men was William Sherley Williams. Most often called "Old Bill," he wandered the western states as a trapper and a scout on the Santa Fe Trail. Soon, other men in search of gold began to roam the area and, after the Civil War, land speculators, anticipating the construction of the westward bound railroad, began to make claims on numerous areas in northern Arizona, including what would soon become Williams. Attracting sheep and cattle ranchers, the settlement was founded in 1876, taking Bill

Williams' name. In 1882 the railroad arrived and, soon, Williams became the shipping centre for the nearby ranching and lumber industries.

Williams gained a reputation as a rough and rowdy settlement filled with saloons, brothels, gambling houses and opium dens. Restricted by a town ordinance to Railroad Avenue's "Saloon Row," it didn't stop the numerous cowboys, railroad men and lumberjacks from frequenting these many businesses.

Even back in those days, early tourists travelled to the Grand Canyon via buckboards and stagecoaches. The Santa Fe Railroad extended its line from Williams to the Grand Canyon making the town the true "Gateway to the Grand Canyon." In 1926, Route 66 was completed through Williams and new businesses sprung up along the highway, which, ultimately, shut down the rail service in Williams in 1968. The train was later reinstated and brings thousands of passengers every year to the Grand Canyon on a fun steam locomotive journey.

Williams was the very last Route 66 town to be bypassed by I-40 in 1984 and, like other Route 66 towns, it suffered, but because of its proximity to the Grand Canyon, not to the same degree as many other small towns along the Mother Road.

A further slight climb brought me the most welcome of traffic signs – the one that warned trucks of a steep descent. It was sixteen miles of mainly effortless downhill riding to Ash Fork, a small town of less than four hundred. I felt I'd gone far enough. The gathering black clouds said one thing – "don't push your luck!" There was a KOA just off the interstate here and I could imagine the price was about thirty dollars. The Ashfork Inn, a nondescript motel on the west end of town was worth trying. Twenty-nine dollars! I nearly took her hand off. The weather didn't matter now – and the lightning had begun. The girl on the desk said I'd have about an hour before the storm broke and there was a gas station across the interstate where I could get food. The only downside was that my room was on the upper floor. I wasted no time stripping the bike and carrying my kit to the sparse, tired room. Two minutes to the gas station and I even had a beer, before heading back to my room past the yards where flagstones are produced – the only business in town, self-styled the "flagstone capital of the world". Television delivered nothing. The shower was hot and I got the day's dust off my body before studying the map for the next day. It looked bleak and I could understand why Steinbeck kept his people moving. I'd arrived in a town that, on first viewing, would make one wonder why it might support a hotel, why indeed the town itself might exist at all. The dust from quarrying of flagstones was only kept down by last night's rain and there was no business being done. Of course, no business had really been done since November 1977, when a big fire destroyed most of the downtown businesses. The Interstate, passing by, sealed the deal – it was, to all intents and purposes, another ghost town.

Day 31 Thu 30 Jun
Ash Fork AZ to Kingman
Distance 181 kms /113 miles
Total so Far 3466 kms / 2166 miles
Accommodation: $43.00 Hotel 6

It was one of those days that starts out miserably – and then sorts itself out. I'd been very lucky in that there hadn't been many. I left Ash Fork with every intention of pitching my tent at Peach Springs, sixty-two miles away, or at Grand Canyon Caverns, some twelve miles closer, if I didn't feel that strong. It had rained heavily overnight and the dark clouds occupied my thoughts while I had a coffee and muffin at the gas station to get me going. At least, it was cool. The map showed a whole lot of nothingness and my route, eight miles out, would diverge from the I-40. I wouldn't even have the dubious company of fast-moving traffic.

Seligman, at the turn of the 20th century, was populated mainly by cowboys working the large ranches in the area. Along with these rough and ready men, came a piece of the Wild West, complete with shootouts on the streets. Saloons and brothels outnumbered the churches three to one. Over the years, Seligman settled down; but, today, is still populated by people working at some of the state's largest ranches. When Route 66 came through, Seligman accommodated the many travellers with numerous motor courts and services, bringing a substantial boost to the town's economy.

The I-40 bypassed the town in the late 1970s and, in the mid-eighties, the Santa Fe Railroad closed its operations in the city. These were tremendous blows upon the small town and it soon came to a slow crawl. Now, it's just a well-preserved tourist stop for those chasing a bit of nostalgia along the Route.

Not having had a proper breakfast before leaving Ash Fork, Seligman made a good place for me to stop to wait out the inevitable downpour. Westside Lilo's diner was busy when I got off the bike there for food. A long table of what looked college students on a summer break, was vocal at this hour of the morning. As the ad goes "Where do they get their energy from?" Sipping my coffee, while waiting for my omelette, my thoughts were distracted by the loud crash of thunder. I might not get further than here today. Drivers wouldn't be able to see through the rain that accompanied the first flashes of lightning, so I settled down, resolved to eat very slowly.

Maybe the weather gods weren't all on my case. The storm passed in an hour and I pulled on waterproofs to get me through the wet remnants of the weather front which, mercifully, was heading for Flagstaff and my rearview mirror. The road was mainly flat after the sharp three-mile climb soon after Seligman. I was on the longest, unbroken, stretch of the original Route 66.

Along the roadside were Burma Shaves signs – small one-liner red signs spaced a few hundred yards apart, designed as early billboard advertising. They served to provide entertainment for motorised travellers along the desolate stretches of the route. Typical examples of the concept might be:

A sign in the middle of nowhere, saying

"A guy Who drives"
Later, another,
"A car wide open"
Still later,
"Is not thinkin'"
And finally,
"He's just hopin'" Burma-Shave

Travellers would entertain themselves trying to come up with the next line before they reached the sign. Most carried a humorous road safety message. They first appeared in 1926, white print on a red background, with a simple and readable font, and remained a major advertising component until the sixties in most of the United States. The first series read: Cheer up, face - the war is over! Burma-Shave. The sign sets I was seeing were recreations of Burma-Shave sign sets installed by Burma-Shave during its original campaigns. Still, original or not, they provided a valuable distraction for me as I covered the miles in ever-warming temperatures.

I pulled into Grand Canyon Caverns for a break. If I'd been a petrol-head, I'd have realised that this place was a monument to America's automotive heritage, although the first impression is of a scrap yard or one of the many roadside motels or attractions that had failed to withstand the arrival, nearby, of I-40 and had fallen on hard times. However, sipping a coke and eating the slice of pie, while looking around the inside of the old building, I realised that, given the right circumstances, I could have lost myself there for days. There were so many bits and pieces – from an oil-can to an old analogue switchboard – that I would have been totally immersed in the fifties. A few people, obviously foreigners, played nine holes of miniature golf in the shadow of towering dinosaurs, while I chilled out in front. They had to be foreigners, because I'd yet to meet anyone who was out enjoying the sun. Greetings I was familiar with from home, like "It's a grand, fine day", totally applicable to the situation I now found myself, with clear blue skies would never be heard here and, if I'd remarked in Seligman earlier that it was "a soft old day", I'd have drawn blank stares.

I took in the information about the place and was surprised that its automobile history well predated the arrival of Route 66. I'd been accustomed to communities being put on the map by railways and the highway and having been local centres, focused on cowboys and lumber before that, but here was proof that the influences of the west coast had stretched inland.

This part of Route 66, in 1914, was on the course for the last of the great Desert Classic races derisively dubbed the "Cactus Derby" by journalists. That race ran from Los Angeles to Ash Fork, before turning south to the finish line in Phoenix, and featured two of the top names in motor sports at that time, Louis Chevrolet and Barney Oldfield.

This would also be the road followed by Edsel Ford in the summer of 1915 as he and friends journeyed west from Detroit to the Panama-Pacific Exposition in San Francisco via the Painted Desert and the Grand Canyon.

A news report of its time read "Williams, Arizona, Thursday July 15, 1915 – Found Cadillac and Stutz crews at Harvey Hotel at Williams waiting for us. All got supplies at garage. Talked to Ford Agent. Got going about eleven. Had lunch at Ash Forks. Loafed along; found it very hot. Bought some gas and oranges at Seligman. Stutz broke another spring about 15 miles out and returned to Seligman. Cadillac and Ford went on to

Kingman, arriving at midnight, Brunswick Hotel. Very rough and dusty roads. Wired Los Angeles Branch for axle parts. Day's run 146 miles."

As an attraction, the caverns themselves date to late 1926, the year of certification for U.S. 66. Legend has it that itinerant cowboy Walter Peck was taking a short cut to a local poker game when he stumbled on and almost into the entrance. After an initial exploration of the cavern, Peck decided to capitalize on his discovery. For ten cents, later a quarter; he would provide tourists with a lantern and lower them into the cavern by rope using a hand crank winch. Among friends, he dubbed this "dope on a rope". A replica of his contraption stands in front of the caverns visitor centre and restaurant.

Route 66 ran a mile or so from "Yampai Cavern" and it took some innovative marketing and promotion to ensure a steady flow of customers. In 1936, utilizing used lumber from the Hoover Dam project northwest of Kingman, a staircase and swinging bridge provided easier access. Following this improvement was the development of a trail system, and a name change to Coconino Caverns.

World War II and gas rationing almost stopped tourism traffic but, like Middlegate Station in Nevada, where I'd stayed in 2014, the cavern proved an attraction for bored servicemen at the Kingman Army Airfield some sixty miles further west and the place managed to remain in business.

The post-war surge in tourism, and the golden age of Route 66 in the 1950's gave rise to dramatic transformation of the caverns complex. It was so popular that the route changed from a two-lane highway, to a four-laner just outside the entrance – and changed back almost as quickly. This piece of highway at the entrance to the property was the only multiple lane segment of Route 66 between Albuquerque and Los Angeles, aside from urban corridors in communities such as Williams and Winslow.

Next to the Grand Canyon itself, this was the most visited attraction in the state of Arizona – until the completion of I-40, and the bypass of Route 66 between Seligman and Kingman in 1978, caused business to nosedive and, while the caverns remained open, one by one, components closed – restaurant and then the lounge. The service station and garage followed. Upkeep and maintenance became a hit and miss proposition, and the motel today shows this. The resurgent interest in Route 66 brought an international clientele and, once more, traffic flowed along Route 66. The caverns resort complex, however, languished. Maybe the renewed interest in Route 66 and its roadside gems came too late. Perhaps the range of automobiles had sealed the fate of the roadside attractions as travellers seemed to experience the "best" of the route through the windshield, the iPad lens and the video apps on their phones. Somehow, I felt that Grand Canyon Caverns was both a reflection of decay and testament to the resilience and vision of successive owners. With modern transportation means, why would anyone bother stopping at a cave, when the Grand Canyon itself was within a few hours' drive – and Las Vegas wasn't far over the horizon? Or maybe that was the romantic in me. Maybe what it really reflected was Einstein's definition of madness – carrying out the same experiment over and over, under the same conditions, expecting a different result. Perhaps Grand Canyon Caverns would always be no more than a footnote to Route 66 – that might need protection.

I headed on to the near-ghost town Peach Springs, in the Hualapai Reservation – a reservation that encompasses more than a million acres, including 108 miles of the Colorado River and a portion of the Grand Canyon. It is the tribal headquarters of the Hualapai Indians and the "People of the Tall Pine" have been occupying the lands for more than fourteen hundred years, where the west rim of the Grand Canyon and the river below, has long since provided food sources and medicinal needs to the tribe. It was from the Haulapai's west rim, that the earliest visitors accessed the wild Colorado River below. Despite being bypassed, Peach

Springs has seen a large comeback, due to the promotions of the Hualapai tribe and their exclusive access to one of the last undeveloped sections of the Grand Canyon. Visitors can tour the Grand Canyon West Rim on the Hualapai Reservation, stay at the Hualapai Lodge in Peach Springs, visit an authentic Native American village, and take a walk on well-known Grand Canyon Skywalk -- a glass bridge that juts out across the canyon, providing views some four thousand feet down to the canyon floor.

All it meant to me was that it had a market store, where I got a turkey wrap and coffee. I didn't feel comfortable and there was no obvious sign of a campsite, though I cycled around, looking.

With nothing marked on the map between here and Kingman, another fifty miles, making the call to carry on from Peach Springs was a major commitment. It would be a good four hours journey and, although it was mainly a drop in elevation, it would be a guessing game as to when I'd get rained on – the clouds were gathering again. It was a beautiful stretch through the high-desert Hualapai Valley along the original route, running parallel to the Santa Fe Railroad tracks to the south. There was no motor traffic apart from the two trucks that passed me going east. The I-40 was much further south.

Just a few more miles down the highway, I passed through Truxton, a ghost town that was born, grew and died with Route 66. Unlike most cities along the Mother Road, this one has no history prior to Route 66. In fact, it started only as a café and a service station in October 1951, when Donald Dilts built the services to accommodate the many wayfarers along the road. Soon other businesses sprung up as competition for Dilts, but sadly, the only ones that remain open today are the nine room Frontier Motel, which was showing a lot of wear – and the Truxton Station. Thanks to the Route 66 Corridor Preservation Program and the Historic Route 66 Association of Arizona, the Frontier Motel's classic neon sign has been rescued to shine brightly for Route 66 generations yet to come.

Hackberry General Store and Visitors' Centre

On the other hand, Hackberry General Store was a sepia-toned postcard, brought to life. The oldest town along this old stretch of the road, Hackberry dates back to a mining camp set up on the east side of the Peacock Mountains in 1874. The Hackberry Silver Mine was soon established and named for a large Hackberry tree growing near a spring adjacent to the mine. Apparently, the rich vein was about 40 feet in width, amounting to large amounts of silver being taken from the mine.

The Hackberry Silver Mine closed in 1919, due to litigation among the owners, but not before it earned almost three million dollars in silver production. After it closed, Hackberry came to a standstill until the arrival of Route 66. Becoming a bit of a tourist town, it hung tight until I-40 bypassed the entire northern loop from the Crookston exit to Kingman.

Today, Hackberry sits mostly silent with the exception of the revived Hackberry General Store and Visitors Centre. Though there's no fuel for sale here, vintage gas pumps sit out front. And the outside is festooned with classic signs and hundreds of pieces of memorabilia. Inside, the store is a virtual museum, where visitors can walk through a vintage diner and see a lifetime collection of Route 66 history, as well as purchasing all kinds of Mother Road souvenirs. Behind a chainlink fence stood a Joshua Tree – so U2 need never sing "I still haven't found what I'm looking for" again.

Valle Vista was shown as having a population of over fifteen hundred people and, more importantly, had a saloon and a good phone signal. It had been a while since I'd been in contact and I ordered a beer and made a call. The adjacent parking lot was only suitable for RVs – I asked – and I realised that I was actually being lazy, not really wanting to get back on the bike for the last seventeen miles into Kingman. I'd have been justified in stopping, because I'd covered nearly one hundred miles, and the rest of the way to town was a single stretch, without a bend. Luckily it was flat, but being able to see the destination from two hours away, brought me back to long days in Colorado and Kansas, when it was hard to maintain motivation in the face of distance that never seemed to diminish.

I resigned myself to getting very wet, certain that the gathering clouds would empty on me before I got to Kingman. As I pedalled, with one eye on the weather, the wind seemed to blow the clouds off my track. I made reasonable time to the city, even though the wind didn't help my progress.

Usually, I choose the first place I see as a stopping spot, but, with rain imminent, and knowing that Kingman was sizeable, I decided to go for the far side of town to make it easy to get out in the morning. It was darkening and, for the last five miles or so, I rode without my sunglasses. The rain started and, just when I thought I'd made a big mistake and the rain got serious, I saw the Motel 6. I wasn't going to look for a campsite. This was going to be a big storm – that might not be gone by tomorrow. I didn't even check the price when I took the room – it was a no-brainer. Forty-three dollars was a good price, even if the room wasn't on the ground.

There was a restaurant next door, so I wouldn't have to travel far. The attractions of Kingman would have to wait for another visit.

A shower and a change of clothes revived me. Two other cyclists were sharing a room just below me. David and Jonathan had met up in the desert and were travelling east together for a few days. Like me, they felt the weather demanded a solid roof. When I met them at the open door of their room, one had stripped his bike and was cleaning and oiling, while the other was cooking up a meal on a camping stove. I was unlikely to have their company in the restaurant for dinner.

A large burger and fries, with onion rings, accompanied by three pints of Blue Moon beer for rehydration, served in an ice-cold glass, was a fitting way of celebrating my longest day, to date, on this trip. Even though the ground had been with me, I felt a great sense of achievement in getting across this stretch of desert. The only question was, would I get to continue the next day. The beer hit me and the food filled me so I was nearly asleep on my feet dodging the rain on the way back to my room. It was cool and fresh from the storm and I was glad – since Flagstaff, I'd dropped nearly four thousand feet. It could get very hot from here.

Day 32 Fri 01 Jul
Kingman AZ to Needles CA
Distance 87 kms /55 miles
Total so Far 3553 kms / 2221 miles
Accommodation: $31.85 KOA

A new month would bring a new state – but, at six in the morning, it didn't look like the latter would materialise. The storm sat above the town and lightning and thunder coincided. The rain brought visibility to feet and I sat at the door of the motel room breathing in the cool air, protected from the elements by the covered walkway of the first floor, while I contemplated the cost of another night here – both in terms of effect on my pocket and on my motivation.

During a seven o'clock lull in the rain, I picked my way through the puddles to avail of the complimentary coffee in Reception. It was vile, so I continued across the road to Carls Jr for a real fast food breakfast.

Back at the motel, I spoke with the other two. David said he'd binned his stove in the desert – "Every town has a Carls Jr – or equivalent!" Obviously, he hadn't yet been to Nevada or Utah. They were thinking about heading off because the forecast seemed to be good. They would try and make it to Seligman and staying on the I-40 would save them fifteen miles. I considered their target to be ambitious as the ground rose all the way. Still, if they managed to have a favourable wind, they'd do it. If the worst came to the worst, there were rest areas where they might, in a pinch, pitch a tent under cover of darkness. I thought that the interstate, though shorter, offered little in the event of mishap. It would be a long day in the saddle, but it would get cooler as they gained elevation. Even the storm might have moderated the temperatures.

Taking my cue from the others, I decided to make a break too. My choices were the same as theirs, but staying on the interstate would add miles to my journey and, anyway, Sitgreaves Pass was the last iconic hill to be climbed to catch up with Steinbeck in Needles. I couldn't miss that one. Nine miles and one hundred and twenty-nine turns, it would climb thirteen hundred feet and would give me a good workout!

Setting off at nine-fifteen, I got to the bottom of the hill in good time, though it required me to ignore the "road closed" sign in the Sacramento Valley. I flagged down a highway maintenance truck coming towards me and asked about the problem.

"Flooding", he said.

"How deep?"
"Too deep for cars. Take your shoes off and stay on the road. You'll be fine – there's no alligators!"
"Thanks!", I said, heading off again.

I worked my way up the hill, slowly, stopping at Cool Springs Station Museum for an expensive bottle of Route 66 Cola. Built in 1926, the initial camp included a café and a Mobil Oil Station. The last stop before the steep Goldroad grade, the camp would have been a welcome break for drivers to check oil, water and gas, and grab a bite to eat.

In the 1930's, The Walker family moved from Huntington, Indiana to operate the camp, improving the station and building eight tourist cabins. However, sometime later, James Walker and his wife divorced, leaving Mrs. Walker and the children to run the camp. The camp flourished and Mrs. Walker remarried a man named Floyd Spidell. After World War II, when people began to travel at a pace never seen before, the chicken dinners served at Cool Camp became famous for the many travellers making their way to California.

In the early 1950's, the Yucca Bypass took its toll on the camp, as well as nearby Oatman, effectively turning it into a ghost town. Though traffic had dwindled on the steep Sitgreaves Pass, the camp stayed in business until 1966, when the entire camp burned to the ground, leaving nothing but remnants of the stone foundations. It was abandoned and neglected. In 1991, it made a brief comeback – rebuilt for the movie "Universal Soldier" – then promptly blown up. The camp was purchased by Ned and Michelle Leuchtner in 2001 and a restoration process was undertaken. In 2004, the Cool Springs Camp station was fully restored, based on old photos.

Cool Springs Station

A twenty-minute break saw me refreshed and ready to take on the twists and turns of the Oatman Road. Previous climbs had prepared me for this and my personal rule – "sometimes three miles per hour is good" kept me going. The flooded road behind would keep traffic at bay and I could meander along the road, taking in the views into the canyons. The sound of asses braying echoed off the rocks. These were the descendants of asses brought in by miners that had, over the years, gone wild. The extent of the previous night's rain was apparent from the silt washed off the hills onto the road. A grading machine worked, scraping inches of mud and pushing it to the edge. It made climbing slippery. In the early days of Route 66, when vehicles had little power, sometimes the only way up the hill was by driving backwards. Driving in the lower gear of reverse solved the problem of early gravity-fed fuel systems. Those who weren't so daring could hire a team of horses to pull their Model Ts to the summit. For others, wreckers who were solely in the area to solve the problem, would haul the stranded motorists over the summit, no doubt making a tidy little profit. Some flatlanders, petrified by the steep incline and winding road, simply paid a local to drive their car over the summit.

Then, I was over the top and looking down to the ghost town of Gold Road below the summit. To the southwest, California and the Colorado River basin with what looked like lush green planted fields, reminded me of staring from the rocky wastelands of southern Lebanon into the irrigated farmland of northern Israel. Nevada stood out to the west. I stopped, astride the bicycle and leaned over the handlebars to stare into the distance ahead. I didn't need to catch my breath, because I was fit at last – and I knew it. I wanted to marvel at the sight that had greeted thousands of travellers making their way west – either to escape their lives forever, or to avail of a few weeks' adventure or fantasy. Ahead was California, my last state. I could look ahead and convince myself that my trip was almost done – that I would, before I knew it, be at the coast west of Los Angeles. I could dream of sipping a cool beer, or a cocktail with an umbrella, at a beach bar, my journey done. But that would have to remain a fantasy. It would be a crazy mistake to ignore the desert I would head into tomorrow. I'd passed through few time zones, many layers of elevation and their attendant climatic challenges. This would be one more. I might as well get stuck in.

I freewheeled downhill over the patched road surface to Oatman – an even quirkier town than Madrid NM. Effectively, a live movie-set, the street was full of tourists – and the wild donkeys they fed. When Route 66 was first built in the 1920s, several supporters worked to have the road parallel the railroad through Yucca, where its supporters lived. However, Oatman was at its peak as a mining community and had more clout. So, even though it made the drive more difficult in old Model-T's, the road took the hazardous journey up Sitgreaves Pass and bypassed Yucca.

By 1930, the town boasted two banks, seven hotels, twenty saloons and ten stores. Over ten thousand people lived in Oatman "area" until the mines were closed during the Second World War, when the government diverted mining efforts to other metal types. Gold would have to wait for better times. Oatman quickly became almost a ghost town as Route 66 was changed to make an easier route south of the mountain passes in 1953. When Laughlin, just across the state line in Nevada, started building up as a popular gambling destination, and Route 66 again became a popular destination for tourists from all over the world, Oatman started coming back to life again.

Oatman AZ

Today, the main street is a line of tourist gift shops and restaurants. Wild burros, descendants of those brought by long ago miners, wander the streets. Gunshots are heard as the Ghostrider Gunfighters perform daily, displaying blazing six-gun shootouts in the middle of Main Street. Jackass Ron's, Outlaw Willie, Bucktooth Burro were names given to businesses here, a recreated Wild West Town. I stopped for lunch and to absorb a bit of tourism. Tour buses, RVs and cars navigated their way around the donkeys, which had right of way and I hoped they received sufficient food from tourists and wouldn't go nosing at my panniers while I ate. An ATM on the wall of a saloon, clearly married the old with the new and the food inside was good. A lone guitarist sang Rock me Mama, Like a Wagon Wheel, for the diners. I had thought that it was a Nathan Carter original, but I was obviously wrong. He was very successful in Ireland, but had hardly cracked Oatman. Apparently, Bob Dylan was the composer. The walls were festooned, in that western tradition, in dollar bills pinned to the pillars. Some carried names of the donors, others not. I've seen different currency notes pinned as decorations behind the bar of some Irish pubs, but nothing to this extent.

With the day marching on, I could only delay for so long and I took out the new map – the last in the Route 66 series. It told me that I had three hundred and sixty miles to go to get to Santa Monica. I'd better get going. Instead of sticking with the mapped route to Golden Shores and Needles, I would go straight for US Hwy 95 and turn south to Needles. It would save me ten miles which, at this stage of the day, when I was euphoric at nearly being in California and over the last mountain pass before the sea, was very welcome. I was also tired from the climb and looked forward to the end of the day. The remaining twenty-two miles to Needles were fine but I had to share Hwy 95 with significant traffic building up for the Fourth of July weekend, heading to Nevada for the gambling or to the lakeshore for the water activities.

Needles Bridge across the Colorado River – the state line to my final state – was worth a stop. I hadn't seen this much water for some time. Needles had almost represented the Promised Land for the Joad family in Steinbeck's work, although they still had the desert to negotiate. Like me, they put down by the banks of the river. They, on the unclaimed river bank, me in the KOA campsite which competed for space with all the other resorts along the south bank. In the 1950s, dams built along the Colorado River, ended a long history of flooding in the region and made the land around Needles suitable for agriculture. This, as well as new recreation opportunities for boating and fishing, gave a boost to the Needles economy. The storm of the evening before had delivered four inches of rain in minutes and had created some flash flooding. It was a measure of how dry the place was that there was no sign of flooding when I got there.

When I-40 threatened to bypass Needles, local citizens worked hard to keep the interstate from missing the town and condemning it to a slow death. Their successful efforts contributed greatly to the town's promising future. From the map, it's clear from the I-40 alignment that Needles prospered at the expense of other locations along Route 66 that might have survived had I-40 been built over Route 66 as it had been in other states.

If I was under any illusion about being on the edge of the desert, the campsite dispelled it. There wasn't a blade of grass in the place. I was driving my tent pegs into gravel, so I used the plastic bag that the bike would be shipped in as a protection between the floor of the tent and the grit on the ground. I spoke with the staff and asked about the weather. They'd had the storm I'd experienced in Kingman the previous night, getting a load of rain. They'd not had rain for five years before that. I said that it was probably to make the Irishman feel at home. There was no rain expected for tonight, though there might be a "bit of a breeze". I didn't like the sound of that and asked if I could have a pitch close to the washroom in case I needed to bail out. The lack of contingency plans on the part of campsites for campers irritated me. They take your money and you're on your own, despite the vulnerability of the accommodation.

I headed off to shower and do my laundry. I had a bit of success in that I only had to pay for drying! I sat and read for two hours in the splendid isolation known to cyclists in a campsite full of air-conditioned RVs. I might as well have been a vagrant. I had a gastronomic delight of baked beans with mashed potatoes followed by a chocolate drink, with a clear view of a majestic sunset!

The advice given to Route 66 travellers is to enjoy the beautiful desert surroundings and the scenic Colorado River before continuing along the Mother Road, but not to forget "you have more than one hundred fifty miles of barren desert ahead with not a single service stop if you take original Route 66, and only a few stops if you take I-40, where you will pay outrageous prices at the gas pumps. Fill up your tank in Needles – better yet, fill it up in Arizona before crossing to California to save a few bucks for a much needed ice cream sundae after crossing the long hot Mojave Desert." What about those of us on bikes?

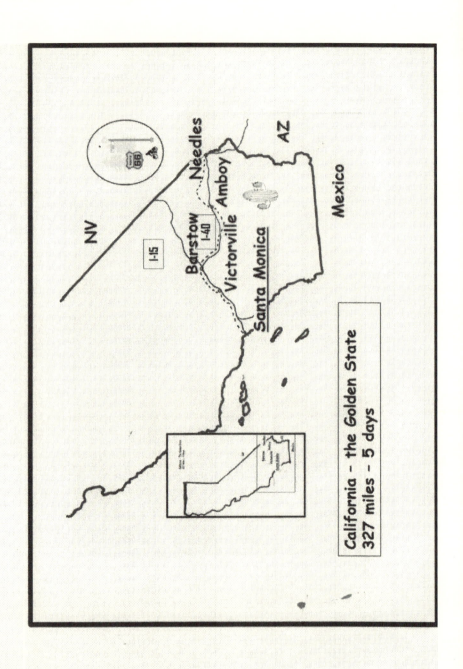

Chapter 8

California – The Golden State

Day 33 Sat 02 Jul
Needles CA to Beyond Amboy CA
Distance 112 kms / 70 miles
Total so Far 3665 kms / 2291 miles
Accommodation: Free – under the desert sky

Last night's sunset guaranteed nothing. At one in the morning, I was packing the tent to take to the washroom for shelter. I barely got there before the rain came down. Two nights of rain in five years – and it happened when I was there! What followed was a light and water show for which I had a ringside seat. Three hours it lasted and I just sat it out. There was nobody likely to come in because the rain was torrential. I reckon that the tent would never have survived it because the campsite was so open. Not a tree – or even a high wall – for shelter.

Pushing the bike to shelter over the open ground of the campsite, I noticed that the dynamo light wasn't delivering light. It put paid to any thoughts I might have had about setting off before dawn to avoid the heat of the day. By four in the morning, the rain had stopped and I just sat there, waiting for the dawn.

Just after five, when I could see enough to distinguish individual colours, I figured it was bright enough to get going. It was my intention to stay on the I-40 all the way to Ludlow and shave some miles off my day. It would still be ninety-two miles. The I-40 killed off one hundred miles of the old Route 66 and left it littered with ghost towns. It meant that, while wild camping might not be a problem, getting water certainly would be. From Goffs near Needles, all the way to Ludlow, where the Mother Road meets again with I-40, the desert is littered with relics from the past and little more.

Following the example of David and Jonathan in Kingman, I stuck with the I-40 to Fenner. Once I'd figured out the problem with the dynamo, I just needed a length of wire to fix it. The shoulder of the Interstate throws up all types of debris so I kept my eyes on the edge of the road and, sure enough, a cable presented itself. I tucked it away until I could find somewhere out of the sun to concentrate on repairing the dynamo setup. Fenner was thirty-eight miles into the day, and I was delighted to get off the interstate and away from the traffic. I missed the experience of imagining how difficult a journey it would have been for those fleeing the Dust Bowl in the thirties. I needed to be on the small roads. With dreams of "beautiful California" and its golden opportunities dancing in their heads, it must have been an incredible let-down to arrive in this sweltering bit of desert on a barren stretch of battered highway.

In Fenner, all roads lead to the Hi Sahara Oasis. Palm trees rising from the desert provide some respite from the heat and water gurgles from fountains. It was only ten-thirty, but, already I was feeling particularly hot and bothered. I ordered breakfast – a beef sandwich, with a bit of salad on the side, two hardboiled eggs and a banana, washed down with coffee. Thirteen dollars! The sign at the cash register set the tone for those surprised by the price "Don't even think of complaining. There's nothing for one hundred miles and it's YOUR choice to choose this place."

This would have been a good time to fix the dynamo. There was a table outside at which I could unload the bike. I cut the cable to strip the wires and found it was an audio cable, with not enough copper for me. It was of no use and I'd have to wait for a bikeshop. I asked a gang of bikers who were loading up on the forecourt, if they might have a bit of scrap wire in their toolboxes, but with no success. I'd just have to carry on. I had enough water to see me through – even if I broke the day, but I was going to stay on the National Trails Highway/Route 66 to Chambless. It was almost thirty miles away, but at least the ACA maps indicated a food stop there. I'd just take it easy and try not to overheat.

I was turning the pedals again at eleven. The day would get to its hottest at about four o'clock and it would be great to get off the road by then. But the question was, where would I stop? There was nothing on the map. For a ghost town enthusiast, this old stretch of the road would be a dream come true with all the crumbling buildings and photo opportunities, courtesy of the passage of the I-40. But there are no roadside attractions, ice cream possibilities, curio stands, or open gas stations, restaurants or motels along here. It was a desert – without relief.

Chambless used to have a gas station, a cafe and several cabins. These buildings are still intact behind a tall wired fence. This one-time oasis in the desert was a popular spot for the long ago travellers of the Mother Road, as it was one of the few places with trees, and the gas station and market once sported a wide covered porch to shade the weary travellers. Not now. The Road Runner's Retreat, which once provided a welcome respite during the long hot drive across the Mojave Desert was equally derelict.

At what had to be the food stop shown on the map, there was no sign of life. Plastic bollards, stood between me and shade. I pushed the bike past this barrier and sank down against the shady wall of the shut store, depleted. I had plenty of food with me and water wasn't an issue either. I just needed to get off the road for a while. An old man appeared in a golf cart from behind an RV on site – with a shotgun on the seat beside him.

He was, initially, quite hostile and ranted about me being on private property and why did I move past the entrance. Who did I think I was and where the hell was I going anyway – except he peppered his rant with profanities. I told him my story, that I wasn't a threat, that I just needed shade. "Get under a fucking bridge so", was his answer. I asked if I could just sit in the shade long enough to get a bit of food and let my water bottle cool a little. I wouldn't make a mess or anything. "How old are you?" he asked. When I said I was sixty, he said "You should have more fucking sense, cycling across the country at your age." He said, "I'm nearly eighty, broke my leg, bust my back, shit, I even got cancer in my prostate. But as long as I got my Viagra…" A slight touch of machismo, I thought. Then, something gave and he mellowed – slightly. My water was too hot to drink and he said he'd open up to let me buy water. Then he just said not to go beyond the shade. He said that if people were dumb enough to bike across the country in this heat, they got what they deserved. It was their own lookout and he took no responsibility for their welfare. Most would have said "You're crazy!" in a grudgingly respectful way. This guy gave me the impression that he felt that, perhaps, the gene pool would benefit from removal of people like me. He didn't see himself as a Good Samaritan – but he still opened the shop for me. I got four bottles of water and a Gatorade as a treat, and he left me to get the stove going. Then it dawned on me that I had the camera charger in my pack. It had a mains cable that I had never used. I could butcher it to give me the length of cable I needed. Things were looking up and already, I felt better. I was accomplishing something.

I used duct tape to secure the new piece of wiring on the dynamo. With a spin of the wheel, there was light and I was happy. Amboy was just eleven miles away and I would normally travel that distance at a sprint – but not today. The temperature had to be well over one hundred degrees Fahrenheit. I got back on the road and, wearily, climbed on the bike.

It was one of those days, the first I'd experienced, where I fantasised about a car stopping and asking if I needed anything. Normally, I'd take the high moral ground in my own mind and convince myself that, if that happened, I'd take pleasure – and strength – from declining assistance. In this case, I was not interested in heroism – I needed help. I pedalled along and a car passed, slowed down and some college kids screamed out the window at me. A beer can flew past me and the car took off again. I was dispirited and shaken. It must have been the heat, because these things wouldn't normally have fazed me.

Another car slowed and pulled in just ahead of me. A man and a woman got out and I stopped. They asked if I was alright – if I needed water. I said I'd plenty, but it was too hot to drink. Dylan introduced himself and his girlfriend, Tess. Then he took a cold bottle of Cherry Cola from the trunk and gave it to me. I didn't know whether to drink it, or just cradle its coolness to my neck.

Dylan and Tess from Connecticut

He took everything out of the cool bag he had there and poured the remnants of the ice and the cold meltwater into my bottles. I was safe again. I drank the cola and we chatted. They were from Connecticut and I said I'd passed through Middletown in 2014. Dylan was a cyclist and knew Gary from the Pedal Power bike shop there, who'd fitted new tyres for me. It's a small world.

I was feeling so much better and Dylan and Tess left me to go on their way. I pedalled the last few miles to Amboy – where Roy's Café didn't serve food. It was a gas station which sold snacks. I'd been thinking about here as a possible stop, but right now it was about getting out of the sun.

Roy's Café and Motel – that was really neither

I had a Gatorade and asked, Mannie, the man running Roy's Motel and Café, if there was somewhere I might camp. "Anywhere, the desert's yours." There was a strong wind that would have been at my back if I'd carried on, but by now, I was broken and disillusioned and couldn't face the bike in this heat – it was one hundred and ten degrees.

The wind was too strong to pitch the tent so I hung out under the shade of the forecourt. People came and went and, every now and again, I'd read the temperature – no change. A girl also seemed to be more than a passing visitor, but somehow seemed like she didn't belong there. I asked if she was marooned and she told me she was from a European University in Geneva, carrying out a project on water – or lack of it. She said all the water from the tap was salty. There was a small desalination plant for showers but drinking water had to be brought in. She was in the last week of a three-week stint and it seemed to me that she'd be glad to go home. I could imagine that there would be some difference between an Alpine valley and the Mojave Desert!

Over the years, the station, motel and cafe served thousands of customers who would rave about Roy's burgers and the service that they received along that desolate stretch of Route 66. In those days, Amboy was an oasis in the desert where hot and tired travellers could stop for food, a cool drink, mechanical services, and gas, delivered with a big smile and a kind voice at Roy's Cafe and Motel. It's been closed for a number of years and the reopening of the café is the start of a dream to open up the whole complex again at some stage.

a car at six o'clock pulled up to the pumps and a girl pulled up in. She needed a can of gas for her boyfriend who was stranded on the interstate. We chatted briefly as Manny filled the can. As she was leaving, she said she might see me when she passed back through in an hour.

That was the point at which I knew that, if I camped in Amboy, I might not get back on the bike the next day. I was in a dark place and I needed to get out of this slump. My experience of the heat today was such that I was scared of the desert – or, rather, of my weakness. I had to face it or stop. Since stopping wasn't an option, at seven o'clock, with the temperature down to a balmy one hundred and six degrees, I pushed the bike out onto the asphalt and rolled on down the highway towards the Pacific – wherever that might be. Ludlow was twenty-nine miles away. I wasn't going to make but I had to cut the cord with Roy's Motel and Café.

For an hour, I cycled, conserving the water I'd bought from Mannie, until dusk began to fall. I looked around and saw a multitude of camping possibilities – as Mannie said, the desert was mine. Finally, too tired to go further, I pushed the bike off the road about fifty yards, and found a flat spot a little higher that the surrounding area. It had a bit of a scrub bush fronting it and I used the bike bag as a footprint again. There was no likelihood of a storm, so I didn't add the flysheet to the tent. Inside, I unzipped all the vents so I only had the mesh between me and the sky. I ate a tin of beans, a little warm from having rested in my backpack and went to bed. It had been an emotional rollercoaster of a day – the kind of experience that turns a road trip back into adventure. I was glad it ended well – that I was off the bike, safe and in a place where I could absolutely relax and get my emotional self back on an even keel.

As night fell, the absence of light pollution displayed the skies in all their splendour. Perhaps a few cars passed on the road during the night and, perhaps a train had passed on the railroad half a mile north of my spot. I was in a ghost town called Bagdad – of which nothing remained – and I was in my sleeping bag. I wasn't hungry and I had enough water. Those who would plan a trip like this – and who would only consider motels for accommodation – might have thought my position to be precarious, but I felt totally safe. I had survived the day and I felt my emotions were back in balance. I was as exhausted as I'd ever been, but I was confident that I'd wake up strong again. I felt relieved – but also felt that I was back on track. It was for moments like this that we suffered. It was worth the pain – though whether or not we'd choose the pain is quite a different matter.

Day 34 Sun 03 Jul
Beyond Amboy CA to Newberry Springs CA
Distance 97 kms /61 miles
Total so Far 3762 kms / 2352 miles
Accommodation: $15.00 RV Park

I slept well. Perhaps it was because I was exhausted, strung out and without options or alternatives that I had no worries about animal or human intervention. The mesh on the walls of the tent was secure against wildlife which would normally avoid human contact. My bags were about ten yards away from the tent so anything drawn to them wouldn't come near me. I hadn't checked to see if snakes or scorpions hung out hereabouts so I had to assume they did and I kept my shoes inside the tent. All in all, when I woke at four-thirty, I felt OK – rested, reassured as to my mental and physical state and ready to go on.

It would be uphill almost all the way to Ludlow, fifteen miles away, where I might get back in touch with civilisation. The I-40 would come back to meet me there. My legs were tired and sore with early morning stiffness, but that would disappear as I pedalled along and loosened them up. It was almost as if my body was aware that the trip was nearly done and since it had stayed quiet up to now, it was asserting its right to be noticed. I felt lethargic, but that was just sleepiness, I convinced myself. Ludlow promised a diner and food.

Ten minutes in, I met Brad, from Milwaukee, coming from the west. Travelling light, with only rear panniers, he'd left Ludlow in the dark to try and get back on the aggressive Route 66 target he'd set himself. He hadn't realised the toll the couple of days riding in the desert could take. It was no big deal, he said, because, if he ran out of time near St Louis, he'd just put the bike on Amtrak – and go home. I admitted that I'd felt, yesterday, that if I hadn't gotten back on the bike, I might have been doing something similar.

Brad rolled off down the road, the fall of ground and significant wind in his favour. I convinced myself that the stiff breeze would, at least, keep me cool. With the elevation gain, I allowed three hours to get to Ludlow – I got there in two-and-a-half. It added to my confidence. Realistically, that was about what it should have taken – but I wanted to make myself feel good!

I headed straight for the Route 66 Diner and ordered a big glass of iced water and coffee, while I studied the menu. A Denver Omelette with sourdough toast and a large OJ was just what the doctor ordered! Just keep the iced water coming! Michelle, my server, kept coming back with liquids.

I felt totally rejuvenated leaving, and crossed to the gas station to buy a few litres of water. I chatted with a group of Canadians who'd shipped their motorbikes down and were touring Colorado, Nevada and part of California. They claimed exhaustion just looking at my bike. "You get used to it", I said – not even believing my own lie.

The National Trails Hwy ran parallel to my old friend, the I-40 to Newberry Springs, a relatively short hop away. It was horrible. The surface had been weathered into what seemed like cobbles, such were the gaps in the asphalt. I regretted my decision but, even worse, I was a prisoner. There was no way off it and what I'd thought were junctions, were only crossings. Eight miles out, I could see that someone had made an unofficial track from my road to the shoulder of the interstate. It was almost as if someone had said "To hell with this for a game of cowboys!" – and brought a dozer out after dark. They'd obviously been as desperate as I was, so I followed their example. And I broke free. Wheeling the bike down the incline, I was relieved. Every crack in the tar had been a worry that I'd puncture, that the tyre might burst or that a spoke might break. It had been nerve-wracking.

Once on the shoulder, I moved along in relative comfort. There was a rest area two miles ahead and I was only six miles from my destination – but, hey, shade is shade.

Just then, a wobble told me that the back wheel had gone soft. It had been inevitable – with the bad road and, then, the transition to the interstate across rough ground. I checked the tyre to see if I'd make it to the rest area – no way. I stripped the bike and got the back wheel off. Luckily, I didn't have to go digging in my pack for a tube – there was one to hand in the bar bag. I ran my finger around the inside of the tyre and felt the dreaded tyre wire. Once I pulled it out, I felt that the replacement tube would be fine – as long as there wasn't another bit of wire. That would be most unlucky. In spite of the mid-morning heat, I managed the repairs well and soon, Surly was reloaded and I headed down the road in a silent self-congratulatory mood. I was in good form when I arrived at the rest area – where no drinking water was available.

I just sat in a bit of shade and wrote up my journal. A couple at the next table offered me water, apologising for it not being cold – as if I cared! It was cool enough to make a difference. They were going home to Southern California after a family gathering in Colorado. I wished them well and Margie insisted in getting a photo with me and the bike. She was really interested in the fact that I was writing my journal in pen and ink rather than keeping electronic notes. I explained that the feel of the pen between my fingers – and the physical turning of pages as I filled them in my journal – gave me a feeling of connection with the trip and, at the same time, a sense of progress. It was almost as if I was physically cataloguing memories, I said. I said I also found it a good way of engaging with people at stops – or not engaging, if that was how I was feeling. Margie said she envied me. She and Tom were about my age and had farmed all their lives. She'd love to take off on a bike trip, but she understood that she was probably too rooted to the land. Instead, she got her "fix" from an annual trip in the RV. I had "The Grapes of Wrath" on the table beside me and Margie said that she'd read it. Being from Southern California, she'd felt obliged to read as much of Steinbeck as possible. Her people were fruit-growers and she felt that Steinbeck didn't give that segment a fair crack of the whip – but, maybe he was right. That was a different time. Now, it was an industry fuelled by migrant labour. It was what allowed fresh fruit to be available widely – instead of being a luxury. What would you think of Trump's idea to build a wall between the US and Mexico? "I'm from SoCal – I don't vote Trump", Margie spat. I said it wouldn't matter to most people in Middle America – I hadn't seen fresh vegetables, since I left Chicago. "They might not realise", Margie said, "that even canned fruit must be picked!" We said goodbye, with Margie promising to look up my "Travels with Surly – Cycling across the USA" online. I thanked them and they left for home. I rested my head on my arms and dozed for half an hour, before following them back on the road.

The Mobil gas station on the exit to Newberry Springs was a fitting place to take a brief halt for a coke. I was due it – and it was cheaper than water. I delayed going to the RV Park, I suppose, because I'd be on my own for long enough. I was alone here, sitting at a table outside the Indian-run fast food outlet attached to the gas station. Everything about the place looked tired and worn out. If it reflected the spirit of the people – and the girl rummaging in the trash can for used plastic bottles for resale, seemed to indicate that it did – I wanted to move along quickly. Newberry Springs has long been a source of water in the dry Mojave Desert. Though the town wasn't founded until 1911, the wagon trains heading to California on the old Mormon Trail in the mid 1800s made this place a regular stopping point along their travels. Located on an ancient lake, it sits on a large basin of underground water, the first water point for wagon trains west of the Colorado River. So, it was a desert, with its life underground and very little above – to paraphrase the song by America.

Wearily, I continued the last couple of miles to the RV Park across the interstate, where Toni, the manager, gave me site number eight. It was an RV site, but it had a bit of shade – a scarce commodity on this park. It would protect me from the wind that was due later. There was no electrical hook-up included and when I asked if I might charge my phone in the restroom, she said "Only while you're there – I wouldn't leave it unattended!" That only reinforced my view of the whole area. Barstow was only twenty-five miles away and I could only imagine travellers checking the fuel gauge to make sure they had enough fuel to get past Newberry Springs.

I handed over the fifteen dollars and pitched my tent and dozed in my chair in the shade, before finally heading off for a shower. There was no laundry, but at least the water was hot and not on a timer. The washrooms were tiny and I hoped there wouldn't be a storm – I'd get claustrophobic in here if I had to take cover! Perhaps I'd become accustomed to the KOAs.

Despite my misgivings, I went back to the gas station for food. It was a case of needs must! There's not a lot that can be done to chicken strips and fries. Still, it would keep me going until morning. When the light went down, I plugged my stuff into the hook-up on the next vacant pitch and got my stuff charged. Fireworks, in advance of the Fourth, began about nine and I had a view from the door of my tent. It was a good effort from a small community. I was lulled by the sound of traffic passing on the interstate. I knew that I was getting up at four – to be on the road at five – but sleep still didn't come easily.

Day 35 Mon 04 Jul
Newberry Springs CA to Victorville CA
Distance 109 kms /68 miles
Total so Far 3871 kms / 2420 miles
Accommodation: $20.00 Shady Oasis RV Park

I was on the road on schedule, feeling happy with myself. It was still dark and I felt I'd have a good day in the saddle. I turned onto what I thought was Route 66, once I'd crossed over the I-40 and found myself on "cobbles" again. It later transpired that I should have taken the next road – then I wouldn't have suffered the puncture. I knew it was going to happen and braced myself with every turn of the pedals. I should have gone on the shoulder of the interstate, but I thought it wasn't bright enough to be seen – despite my newly functioning lights. The time I'd gained by the early start was swallowed up in waiting for a degree of light to change the flat. So I arrived at the Chevron gas station after only five miles and one hour's travel, feeling irritated.

Time for a coffee. I was thinking that if there was likely to be a celebration of the Fourth of July, maybe a short day to a big town might be in order. Barstow had a population of over twenty-two thousand so it might be good. I asked two locals what might be going on there today. "Drinking and more drinking – so if'n you don't like drinkin', yed better cycle thru', quick as ye can. And get off the road early 'cos them drunks gotta get home." That summary was good enough for me. It didn't inspire stopping.

Daggett seemed to be one big Marine Corps Base and, as I cycled past, it showed all the activity of a Wednesday afternoon in the Curragh Camp in Ireland during the eighties. Perhaps it was the holiday. I passed into Barstow eight miles further on – and said goodbye to the I-40 – and the Joad Family of Steinbeck's imagination. Ma Joad would say, when they arrived in the government-run camp: "We're Joads. We don't look up to nobody. Grampa's grampa, he fit in the Revolution. We was farm people till the debt. And then—them people. They done somepin to us. Ever' time they come seemed like they was a-whippin' me – all of us. An' in Needles, that police. He done somepin to me, made me feel mean. Made me feel ashamed. An' now I ain't ashamed. These folks is our folks – is our folks. An' that manager, he come an' set an' drank coffee, an' he says, 'Mrs. Joad' this, an' 'Mrs. Joad' that—an' 'How you gettin' on, Mrs. Joad?'" She stopped and sighed. "Why, I feel like people again." They were on their own road now, to Bakersfield, while I would plough on to Los Angeles – and I would miss their company. I'd read the rest of their story, from a distance.

When I got to Barstow Station at eight-thirty, there was a bit of activity. The McDonalds restaurant dining area is built from railroad cars and it might have been nice to have breakfast in a quirky setting, but I couldn't see how I might keep an eye on the bike. If I couldn't leave my phone unattended in the RV Park at Newberry Springs, I certainly wasn't going to let the bike out of sight here.

Carls Jr was half a mile further on. It had big windows and a place outside where I could lean the bike. The clientele didn't seem animated – there was no indication of an impending national holiday – and I felt the locals in Newberry Springs had been on the money. I got my food, ate it, and replenished my water bottles, before getting back on the road out of town. There was some indication of Route 66 passing through, but I got the feeling that, because it was, in reality, so close to Los Angeles for motor travellers, it didn't inspire stopping. I got the feeling that if you were in Barstow, you were going there. If you were passing through, you kept going. It's located at the junction of three major highways – I-15, I-40 and State Highway 58 in the western Mojave at the entrance to the Mojave National Preserve and is home of the U.S. Army National Training Center, Marine Corps Logistics Base, NASA's Goldstone Deep Space Network and Burlington Northern-Santa Fe Railroad Yards. All in all, it had a strong military connection.

All the way to Helendale, probably a corruption of "Hill and Dale", judging by the topography, there was a bit of a climb, but it was the constant headwind that meant I would never again be able to listen to the Irish radio show, "The South Wind Blows", without thinking about those last days on Route 66. I pulled off the road at Dempsey's Pub and had a coke. I don't think it was even open – or, if it was, I was the only customer. I chatted with the lady behind the bar and I remarked that I hadn't felt comfortable in Barstow. "Desert rats, they are. Trapped with no way out, stuck there, whether they like it or not!" Not exactly a glowing testimonial to the town. I got my water bottles filled again. After the days since Flagstaff, during which I'd had to really conserve water, this was a real luxury.

Molly Brown's was a busy diner down the road a few miles and I stopped for lunch. It was as close as I'd come to a Mom & Pop Diner on Route 66 and the fact that it was busy – and popular with locals – made me order the liver, onions and bacon, served with mashed potatoes and greens, with gravy – and extra gravy on the side. I'd died and gone to heaven. It was the best meal I'd had since the Big Texan steak in Amarillo. Deprivation makes a person remember meals for weeks! I'd considered declaring that I was a Senior – and getting the discount – but imagined that the portion might be adjusted to cater for failing appetites. My appetite certainly wasn't failing so I went for the full Monty! A chat with the couple at the next table, thankfully delayed my exit into the headwind. I had the misplaced optimism that it might die down and leave me alone.

Elmer's Bottle Tree Ranch a few miles down the road is a perfect example of why someone should travel Route 66. There had been many examples of eccentricities along the way – the Cadillac Ranch, Paris Springs Gas Station, The Blue Whale – even Pops. The Bottle Ranch shows one man's passion for creating something unique which has visitors coming from all over the world. It is, literally, a forest of bottle trees (large metal pipes with bottles hanging from them), on the side of the road, right in the heart of the California desert. Elmer accepts donations but it is free to enter.

Elmer's Bottle Tree Ranch

I had known about this place before I started out and I was glad it was so accessible. As I parked the bike against the fence, I knew it would be everything it had promised. It was hard to know what to focus on. Metal poles were set in the ground, with "branches" welded to them and something – it may be a rifle, it may be a rake, sitting like a fairy atop a Christmas tree. Bottles, neck first were skewered on the branches. I spent an hour just wandering around, just being there. It serves no practical purpose, other than taking used bottles out of circulation, but, to me, it was high art. There was so much going on, but I would have needed company to give it its due. He even has a tree made from an old missile! At least ten other people passed through while I was there.

Any eighty-year old pub on Route 66 will have history. The Iron Hog Saloon in Oro Grande began life back in the 1890s and was known as the Butterfield Stage Stop. It was rebuilt in the thirties and has worn a number of hats since then – sometimes a restaurant, a farm machinery dealership, a roadhouse, biker bar, strip club and, allegedly, a house of ill-repute. Roy Rodgers, cowboy singing legend, carved his name in the counter and Johnny Cash sang there. It featured in movies, most notably, Easy Rider and Erin Brockovich. Apart from the blurb, because I was close enough to the end of the day, I had to drop in.

The Iron Hog at Oro Grande

The guy playing the guitar with amplification, like a bad busker on Grafton Street in Dublin, outside the door was appearently just tuning up for a performance later. It was most definitely a bike bar now. Everything screamed "no lycra". Inside, there were four people. A girl inside the bar served me a beer and the two cowboys sitting at the counter looked me over. Both had moustaches, white Stetsons and drank bottles of Corona. The only distinguishing feature was that one had "Boss" and the other had "Foreman" on their shirts.

Turns out that the boss was the current head at the Roy Rodgers Ranch, nearby. It had been the home of the Singing Cowboy and Dale Evans and was available for weddings and functions. "It's back the road a bit" said

Chris Kennedy, the Boss. I asked if it had access to water – I couldn't see any point in owning land up here on the high desert without it – and Chris said it was down by the "river" that had been off to my right as I travelled from Helendale. I said I'd seen a wildfire along that valley as I travelled down, but Chris said it was well away from his place. If he wasn't worried, why should I be concerned on his behalf. We chatted about cycling and he asked how far I'd go in a day. I said it was about hours in the saddle for me and that I tended to max out at about ten. That gave me one hundred miles – without breaks – on a good day. "Same as a horse so", he said. "We cover about thirty-five miles a day, at three-and-a-half miles an hour. I felt I'd established my credibility, because he insisted on buying me a beer and invited me back to the ranch for a tour. I thanked him, but said he had better things to do on the Fourth of July, than to be showing an Irishman around his home. Anyway, I was fairly solid in my plan now for the next few days. I said I was going on to Victorville today.

The other biker-friendly man in leathers and tattoos, at the counter, rang a bike shop in Victorville to see if they were still open. He was the owner and would have asked them to give my bike a full service if I called in. They were closed early for the holiday, but he said the offer was still open tomorrow, if I wanted to avail of it. I'd be gone long before they opened in the morning but I thanked him for the offer and asked him if he could fill my bottles again – he owned the pub too.

It was the kind of place where, if I'd been with someone, I'd have pitched the tent out the back and come back for some real beers. I was due a blow-out! I had just about seven downhill miles – which was just as well as I had to pedal against the wind all the way. The Garmin brought me to the campsite by way of a three-mile detour and a big hill on a very busy D Street.

I paid twenty dollars for a shady spot and pitched the tent, inflated my sleeping mat and pillow and promptly lay down for an hour. Going for a shower, I mistakenly went into the female's washrooms. Good job there was no one there. It had been a long day!

Day 36 Tue 05 Jul
Victorville CA to Claremont CA
Distance 107 kms /67 miles
Total so Far 3978 kms / 2487 miles
Accommodation: $73.00 Claremont Lodge

The chill I felt at four in the morning, when I got up to face the second-to-last day on Route 66, was something new. It was a big change from previous days when I'd barely be able to catch my breath. I was facing twenty uphill miles to Cajon Summit, the last obstacle before the coast. It included two thousand feet of elevation gain, so it wasn't to be sneezed at. Preparing my oatmeal reminded me that I needed to replenish my fuel stock so I'd have to find a hardware store along the way. From Cajon Junction, just below the summit on the west side, I would be effectively in greater Los Angeles, although the communities kept their own names.

Six o'clock was time enough to leave and instead of backtracking yesterday's route, I took the nearest ramp to the I-15 and jumped off at the first exit. Then it was uphill, seemingly forever. Victorville, with a population of over one hundred thousand, was stirring itself at that time and, in keeping with other large urban areas I'd passed through at morning time, my sighting of pedestrian traffic was limited to the detritus of society – those without means, some pushing shopping trolleys loaded with personal effects and some with vacant stares as they walked the pavement. It never ceased to make me grateful for what I had, time and means. Regardless of how fragile I might have felt in Amboy, I was there by choice – with a means of escape. These people did not have the same access.

A Walmart alongside I-15 failed to provide fuel, so I just bought a sandwich and coffee to keep me going. The day had warmed up and I relaxed into the climb, drinking water as required. Cajon Pass, which separates the San Gabriel Mountains from the San Bernardino Mountains, was once the only gateway negotiable by wagon trains. The Mojave Trail, the Mormon Trail, and the Spanish Trail converged here. Indians, trappers, explorers and scouts passed on their way to what would become the San Bernardino Valley. The first paved highway was built over the pass in 1916 and was upgraded several times until the highway was replaced by I-15 in 1969.

The last hill!

At the top of the pass at the Oak Hill exit, the historic Cajon Summit Inn, a Route 66 landmark serving customers since 1952 was one of the few survivors along this stretch of highway. I should have taken a picture – it burned to the ground during a California wildfire on August 16, 2016, a month after I'd passed.

The climb hadn't been as bad as I might have expected and from the summit, it was a white-knuckled descent to Devore, where I stopped to catch my breath. The ACA maps showed an alternative, to the main route, along the Van Helen Parkway. This saved about nine miles, bringing me down Sierra Avenue to Fontana, where I joined the Pacific Electric Bike Trail – which, ironically, prohibited electric bikes!

Two hours on this great greenway brought me to Upland and, as an added bonus, I crossed a street beside an Ace Hardware store. I was all fuelled up again. Prior to Upland, I'd been going through industrial and new-development residential areas, but here I emerged into a quaint village main street opposite Paulie's Pizza. It was a no-brainer.

An hour later, I left, lazy and unrushed. Wherever I stopped today, Santa Monica would be within easy reach tomorrow. When I got to Claremont and cycled round this college community, I settled on Hotel Casa 425. It was in the centre of what might be a lively area and I obviously have good taste – they had a special for me for two hundred dollars. It was a bit rich for my taste so I took myself off to motel-land beside the San Bernadino Freeway. The Claremont Lodge fulfilled all my requirements and cost seventy-three dollars. Across the road, the Waba Grill had a sizeable noodles dish for five dollars.

Day 37 Wed 06 Jul
Claremont CA to Santa Monica
Distance 98 kms /61 miles
Total so Far 4076 kms / 2548 miles

Today saw the end of my journey. From Claremont to the coast, I was on some busy but mostly quiet residential or business streets. When Route 66 began, its purpose was to connect the small towns between Chicago and the Pacific Coast. At that time, many of the Los Angeles suburbs were small towns, filled with mom and pop diners, motels, roadside fruit stands, and curio shops. I hadn't seen many of them and this morning was no different.

Knowing I was so close to the end, had a dampening effect on me. I was sluggish. It was as if there was no need to hurry – that Santa Monica Pier would always be there. By my planned schedule, I should have been looking at the climb over Sitgreaves Pass for my first view of California, rather than pushing the bike across the hotel forecourt to McDonalds for breakfast. My planning had been spot on, really. If I'd taken the planned rest days at the end of each map section, I would be about facing into the desert at this stage. I preferred being sluggish, but hindsight is a great thing – I had had an idea of what to expect crossing the Mojave Desert, and I was prepared to face that. But the reality was as difficult a time on the bike as I've ever had.

At McDonalds, I was approached by a young man – probably in his late twenties – looking for assistance. A panhandler, he would have been called in history. I'm not sure if the term is still in use. Anyway, I was on the point of walking past him when I had a thought. Pulling out the bag I kept my laundry change in – I must have amassed fifteen to twenty dollars in it by now – I gave it to him and said "Now, I want you to keep an eye on my bike while I have my breakfast." Immediately, he began to remonstrate, giving reasons why he had to be elsewhere and why he couldn't mind the bike. I reached over, took the bag of coins and told him that the money would only be his if he and the bike were still there when I came out after eating. He was dumbstruck as I walked away.

As it happened, I got a window seat, once I got my order, and brought the bike around into view. I gave the man the money and said I'd only been trying to have him earn it rather than being given it for doing nothing. The lesson was lost on him – but not on me. I suppose that when a person's self-respect has been eroded to the point of having no difficulty begging, philosophical questions about the intrinsic value of work as a good thing in itself, are lost on the beggar. He was living in the moment, while I was trying to give him something to look back on. I went back to my breakfast.

In the rush to California, for which Route 66 was partially responsible, the area around Los Angeles boomed as travellers escaped the dust bowls of the Midwest, attracted to the climate and opportunities that the Golden State provided. Two hundred thousand people used the mother road to go west, initially in search of a better life and adventure, from the Dust Bowl – because things couldn't get any worse. It expanded and sprawled eastwards, as if to extend the hand of friendship to those who'd managed the journey. More likely, it was that people got over the last summit and stopped where the truck broke down.

Die-hard Route 66 fans can still travel along various alignments of the "original" road, as the path continues to exist along a number of thoroughfares all the way to Santa Monica, snaking through suburbs passing from one community seamlessly one into another. From Pasadena, Route 66, on city streets, passes through a number of Los Angeles suburbs and streets variously known as Foothill Boulevard, Colorado Boulevard, Huntington Drive, Sunset Boulevard, and Santa Monica Boulevard to the western end of the Mother Road at the Santa Monica Pier.

Just across the Los Angeles River, beside the entrance to Chinatown, I stopped for coffee at Starbucks. I wanted to slow it down so I'd get to the Pier in the early afternoon. I'd reached LA and the rest was just to finish out the journey. There was nothing remarkable about the last miles to Sunset Boulevard. The end I came into, from Cesar Chavez Avenue, reminded me of arriving into any big city on my route – Tulsa, Oklahoma, Amarillo – tired and depressed looking. I'd had expectations of glitz and glamour. I suppose that faraway hills are greener. The map took me down Fountain Avenue and off the main traffic route. Perhaps, if I'd stayed on Sunset Boulevard, I'd have seen opulence on the street. Instead, I saw opulence on the ground as I was diverted through the residential streets on Beverly Hills, off Santa Monica Boulevard. Perhaps the mansions are elsewhere. All I saw were fine properties, well-maintained, with manicured grass.

I followed the map and, because its purpose was simply to get me to Santa Monica, I passed on sightseeing opportunities of Sunset Strip, Rodeo Drive, and Wiltshire Boulevard and got back on the main drag by Century Park, before diverting onto Broadway. For old time's sake, I stopped off for a large burger and fries at Carls Jr, before the last three miles to the end. I didn't need my first thought at the end to be "Where's the toilet?"

Santa Monica Pier was buzzing with tourists, as I threaded my way through, pushing the bike to get to the sign which said "Santa Monica – 66 – End of the Trail. I was done. I got the picture, met a few bikers in leathers who'd also made the same trip as I had – but faster – and rolled the bike off to get a well-deserved beer and consider the immediate future. I'd learnt, from previous experience, that a journey such as this was too big to be a single entity. Instead, it was a collection of one-day spins. Getting to the pier at Santa Monica was simply another, short, day's cycle – but it was the last one.

Sitting with my beer, I reflected on my trip. Route 66 is a wonderful road trip. Distances between iconic markers are not a challenge to cyclists until they reach New Mexico, coming from the east. Taking the trip in a car would be to catch a snapshot of American life rather than experience it.

My pace allowed me to get a glimpse of the history rather than see the route as a series of connected landmarks, punctuating a distance. I took a trip – as a tourist, not as a researcher. Having completed a distance equal to that from The West of Ireland to Athens, I was conscious that my view of society along the route was of a homogenous population. That view is, no doubt, wide of the mark. To distil the American population into Republican and Democrat is to miss the point that it is a young nation, comprising a cultural melting pot of nationalities – with widely differing views on being "Americans".

In my planning, in order to give myself a purpose for undertaking the trip, I'd really only considered Route 66, from the perspective of Steinbeck's "The Grapes of Wrath". This was skewed and ignored the social meaning of the route in the aftermath of World War II when ease of travel and prosperity fuelled the American dream of travel and adventure. It also ignored the fact that Route 66 only joined up existing routes and that the journey from east to west had been done long before Route 66 came into existence. Cattlemen had opened up the frontier – but had displaced the native population which had been there for thousands of years. Frontierism still lives on in the minds of those in the sparsely-inhabited communities of New Mexico, Arizona and Nevada. Celebrating gun culture is something the liberals in the cities consider to be low-class. It's trotted out as something to which the uneducated subscribe. They deride things – like NASCAR, Mixed Martial Arts and trucks – as definitions of being redneck. Internationally, areas outside cities are portrayed as cowboy country or open-plan meth factories, where observance of the rule of law is dubious. It is this dismissal of the conservative values of communities by the liberal educated classes that has thrown up the likes of Donald Trump – who, instead of being roundly beaten, was still gaining ground. Politics in the US is on television and the winner is the one who harnesses that medium. Television, unless one subscribes to cable, is mindless.

I was reminded of an ancient Native American Lakota proverb, I'd read "Memory is like riding a trail at night with a lighted torch. The torch casts it light only so far, beyond that is darkness." I obviously had a weak torch. My, always onward, movement had an extremely narrow focus. To get deeper into the culture of the land through which I'd travelled would have required time, research and an understanding of the questions that needed to be asked. In hindsight, I regretted not having taken Keith up on his invitation to take a side-trip to Perkins, OK, where time off the bike might have educated me further.

Still, it would be wrong to imagine that I hadn't been educated. To my limited knowledge of US history, the Civil War had taken place in the east and I was unaware that the Civil War had extended as far west – that the battle of Glorieta Pass in New Mexico had been fought to prevent a major effort by Confederate forces to break through to Colorado and California. Major John Chivington, an officer of the Union forces, had had a central role in this battle in March 1862, but, two years later, he would be responsible for leading for leading a 700-man force of Colorado Territory militia during the massacre at Sand Creek, in what is present-day Kiowa County in eastern Colorado, in November 1864 when an estimated seventy to one hundred and sixty-three peaceful Cheyenne and Arapaho – about two-thirds of whom were women, children, and infants – were killed and mutilated by his troops. I'd passed through that county in 2014, without ever having an idea of its history.

I'd only interacted with white Americans along the route – apart from experiencing the generosity of the family in Zuni Pueblo. I hadn't been able to establish the ethnic or cultural background of those early white settlers, whose methods of exploiting the natural resources – agriculture, mining and drilling – had displaced the hunter-gatherer members of the native population. Irish names appeared frequently in the history, but not so much in the modern communities.

Travelling alone on Route 66 is lonely and expensive. Company is everything and the psychological benefits of a conversation cannot be overstated. The absence of city parks open to cyclists as a means of keeping costs down was a problem, but the extensive network of motel accommodation possibilities means that the trip lends itself well to "credit card" touring rather.

There are wonderful people out there. This trip had only reinforced the view I'd formed of American people in 2014. I'd considered the reception I'd received in Chambless, when I'd been at low ebb, to have been an aberration. I'd only had a single moment – beer-drinking college kids on the Fourth of July – when I'd had a negative thought.

Fresh fruit and vegetables were almost unavailable along the route. It makes me worry for the diet of those living in smalltown America, whose financial circumstances might preclude ownership of an automobile. Fast food outlets were never in short supply so hunger might not be as significant an issue as malnourishment or, as a minimum, poor diet.

The crowds around Santa Monica didn't fill me with elation. I'd been in this situation before. In August 2014, I arrived into Georgetown in Washington DC on my bicycle. I felt isolated in the crowds and couldn't wait to get out again. I had the same feeling here and had to leave.

It was only after I'd purchased my flights to and from the United States, that Aer Lingus had instituted its direct flights to Los Angeles. I'd booked to return from San Francisco and I now had five hundred-odd miles to travel to get to the airport. My trip wasn't over. The next phase of my journey would be the pleasure after the pain. I had, as part of my planning, included a trip I might never again have an opportunity to take on. The Pacific Coast Highway, from Seattle to San Diego, is one of the most popular cycling routes in the United States. I was almost seven days ahead of schedule and, if I was to avoid accommodation costs in San Francisco –

I didn't want to wear out my welcome with Henry there – I'd have to slow down. I could drop my mileage to short days, but that would mean early finishes and lots of alone time in campsites. Alternatively, I could begin my days at a more acceptable time of day – say, nine in the morning instead of five. I'd like to have spent time in Santa Monica but, without company or plans, to paraphrase Robert Frost, "For I have promises to keep, and miles to go before I sleep."

EPILOGUE
The Road to the Airport

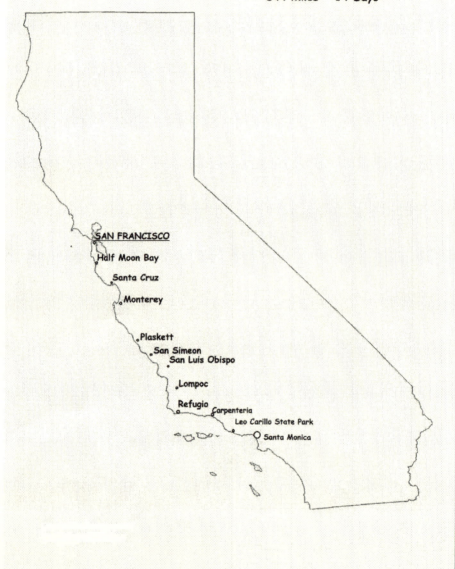

For the next fourteen days, in payment for not having availed of scheduled rest days, I meandered my way up the West Coast, from the campsites of State Beaches at Leo Carrillo, Carpenteria, Refugio and New Brighton to hostels in Monterey and Santa Cruz. I stayed in motels in Lompoc and San Luis Obispo. I took time off in Refugio to enjoy the beach, Monterery to get a feel for Steinbeck's place and in Santa Cruz to slow down my approach to San Francisco. Averaging fifty miles a day when I was probably at my fittest, doesn't, in hindsight, make a lot of sense. It gave me more hours off the bike than I would have liked, but it prepared me for re-entry into settled society.

My friends, Danielle and Henry, with whom I'd cycled for a time in Nevada and Utah in 2014, drove down the coast to renew our acquaintance in Ventura and cycle with me for a couple of days. I enjoyed these days immensely and it showed me that I'm not as comfortable in my own company, exclusively, as I might have thought. Long evenings spent alone are all very well when the company is Steinbeck's work, but there is absolutely no substitute for good, human, like-minded company.

The Pacific Coast Highway from Santa Monica to San Francisco, is as different from Route 66 as it is possible to get. Popular with bike tourists coming from the north, there was never an evening without company – or, at least, the possibility of company. Meeting fellow cyclists on the road became so common that the thrill of a chance meeting lost its lustre. The traffic was ever-present and, though the roads were good and drivers, considerate, I sometimes felt wishful for the quietness of frontage roads in Texas, New Mexico and Arizona.

The abiding memory I will take from this "road to the airport" is one of comfort. The harshness of the road west disappeared into the soft countryside of coastal California and, in those I met, privilege replaced struggle. Perhaps it was because those I encountered were, in the main, tourists – myself included – and were where they were by design rather than by necessity, that I got that impression.

When I finally reached San Francisco, the key to Henry's apartment in my pocket, I knew that my cycling adventures in the United States were probably over. I would have to concentrate on finding out what would lie along a route of similar distance in Europe and realise that I need to research more before setting out if I want to achieve more from what is never "just a bike tour".

Appendix

The Packing List:

This list arose from "lessons learnt" on my last trip. It is always a work in progress. Deciding on the layout and distribution of the kit was a scientific matter – the heavier stuff in the front panniers and balanced left to right. This changed over the course of the trip as items migrated to more accessible locations.

Front Left: Kitchen, food and medical
Front right: Library (maps, journal, pens, etc), Repair kit and Rain Jacket
Rear Left: On-bike clothing, bike bag and Sleeping bag
Rear Right: Off-bike clothing Spare shoes, and sleeping mat
Bar Bag: Cash, passport, flight details, phone, journal and contact lists

Bike
Surly Long Haul Trucker
Brooks Flyer Saddle
Surly Nice front rack, Tortec rear racks
Dynamo Hub
Ortlieb Classic Roller Panniers (Front & Back)
Cheap Frame Bag
Altura Bar Bag

Camping gear
Jack Wolfskin eVent II tent
Quecha one-season sleeping bag
Silk Sleeping bag liner (gives another 5 degrees protection?)
Salewa speeping mat
Small light for tent
Clothes line and safety pins
REI Flex-lite chair
Mini Trangia Stove + lighter
Fuel
Cutlery & cup, Chopping Board
Water bottle x 3

Cycling Clothes
Helmet, glasses and gloves
Merino wool base layer (long sleeved)
Short-sleeve tops x 2
Cycling underwear x 2
MTB Shorts x 1
Long-fingered gloves
Socks x 3 prs
Buff x 2
Gilet
Rain Jacket
Waterproof leggings

Off-bike clothes
Long trousers
Shorts
Shirt x 2
Swimming trunks
Underwear x 2
Warm socks x 2 (for morale)
Sandals
North Face Thermal jacket

Toiletries
Towel
Washcloth
Soap/Shampoo
Toilet paper
Wet wipes
Toothbrush + Toothpaste
Shaving brush, Soap and razor

Bike Tools
Pump, Replacement tubes, Puncture kits, Tyre levers,Chain Lube
Nuts, bolts, screws,Allen Keys, Multi-tool, Chain Tool + spare links,
Swiss Army Knife, Pedal Wrench, Zip Ties, duct tape

Documents
Passport, Cash, Credit Card, ATM/Debit card, Flight Reference, Travel insurance card, Contacts lists, Small lock for hostels etc.
Electronics Garmin eTrex 20, Cateye computer
Irish Phone, Verizon Jetpack plus cables and US plug
Camera (plus charger and cable

Library
Maps, Journal & Pens, Waterproof bag, John Steinbeck's The Grapes of Wrath

Medical Box
Person medication, Sunscreen, Lip balm, Mosquito repellent, Sudocream (or equivalent
Diorolyte rehydration sachets
Misc plasters, Scissors, Sewing kit

Distances and Accommodation Costs

Day	To	Distance	Accommodation	Cost
		Illinois		
1	Elwood	125 km	Public Park	Free
2	Towanda	91 km	Town Park	Free
3	Divernon	174.3 km	Private Park	Free
4	St Charles	166.1	House Guest	Free
		Missouri		
5	Stanton	111 km	KOA	$28.75
6	Devil's Bend	114.6 km	House Guest	Free
7	Marshfield	122 km	RV Park	$15.00
8	Carthage	159 km	Guest Motel	$51.00
		Oklahoma		
9	Vinita	136 km	RV Park	$10.00
10	Tulsa	112 km	Stealth	Free
11	Davenport	104 km	RV Park	$12.00
12	El Reno	138 km	Budget Motel	$50.00
13	Clinton	116 km	Campsite	Free
14	Elk City	32 km	KOA	$27.00
		Texas		
15	Shamrock	118 km	Campsite	$3.00
16	Groom	91 km	Chalet Inn	$63.95
17	Amarillo	104 km	KOA	$28.00
18	Adrian	94 km	RV Park	Free
		New Mexico		
19	Tucumcari	104 km	House Guest	Free
20	Santa Rosa	0 km	Campsite	$19.95

Day	To	Distance	Accommodation	Cost
21	Romeroville	100 km	KOA	$27.50
22	Madrid	149 km	Ballpark	Free
23	Exit 140	114km	Casino Hotel	$100.00
24	Grants	106 km	KOA	$27.75
25	Zuni Pueblo	116 km	Church Mission	Free

Arizona

26	Chambers	77 km	Days Inn	$70.00
27	Holbrook	118 km	KOA	$27.85
28	Meteor Crater	100 km	RV Park	$28.75
29	Flagstaff	67 km	Du Beau Hostel	$69.00
30	Ash Fork	85 km	Ash Fork Inn	$29.00
31	Kingman	181 km	Hotel 6	$43.00

California

32	Needles	87 km	KOA	$31.85
33	Mojave	112 km	Desert	Free
34	Newberry	97 km	RV Park	$15.00
35	Victorville	109 km	RV Park	$20.00
36	Claremont	107 km	Motel	$73.00
37	Santa Monica	98 km		

| **Total** | | **4076 km** | | **$871.60** |

Made in the USA
Columbia, SC
10 April 2018